Bluestones and Salt Hay

Bluestones and Salt Hay

AN ANTHOLOGY
OF CONTEMPORARY
NEW JERSEY POETS

Edited and with an introduction by

Joel Lewis

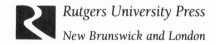
Rutgers University Press
New Brunswick and London

Acknowledgments appear at the end of the book.

Copyright © 1990 by Rutgers, The State University
All rights reserved
Manufactured in the United States of America

This book was designed by Karolina Harris. It was set in Electra with Berkeley Old Style display type by G & S Typesetters, Inc. The printer/ binder was Bookcrafters, Inc., of Chelsea, Michigan. All materials used in this book are acid-free.

Library of Congress Cataloging-in-Publication Data

Bluestones & salt hay : an anthology of contemporary New Jersey
  poets / edited, and with an introduction, by Joel Lewis.
      p.   cm.
  ISBN 0-8135-1485-1 (cloth)—ISBN 0-8135-1486-X (pbk.)
   1. American poetry—New Jersey.   2. —New Jersey—History—Poetry.
3. American poetry—20th century.   I. Lewis, Joel.   II. Title:
Bluestones and salt hay.
PS548.N5B55   1990   89-36067
811'.540809749—dc20   CIP

British Cataloging-in-Publication information available

IN MEMORY OF
TED BERRIGAN
(1934–1983)
and
JOSEPH CERAVOLO
(1934–1988)

Contents

Foreword

My father was in the War in Germany in 1945 and because my mother had little family of her own, when the time came she went to his family in Milleville, New Jersey, to give birth to me. My grandfather was a glassblower at the Whitall-Tatum factory there. We used to spend summers at nearby Union Lake with frequent visits to "the shore." I remember what seemed like long bus rides from New York through industrial New Jersey. I remember how distinct things seemed out the window and how one got past "the city" and progressed fairly quickly. I remember the sense of getting closer to fresh air, real America, open spaces, the sea. It was very different from taking the D train to Coney Island.

In New York City, where I was growing up, everyone seemed to be from elsewhere. In New Jersey, however, people seemed to be from New Jersey for one or two generations. Yet they were as various as all the people in New York were. Maybe they weren't holding onto their identities so much in New Jersey. My father's people were German on one side—"black" Irish, Scots, English mix on the other. My great-grandfather, also a glassblower, had come over from Bremen in 1850. My cousin in Vineland had married an Italian boy, a car salesman. My brother in Teaneck had married a Jewish woman, a musician and teacher.

What was the quality back then that was quintessentially New Jersey? Simplicity? I remember a black family crossing the railroad tracks with a picnic basket in the early fifties somewhere near Bridgeton. I remember my father rowing an old wooden boat, blending in perfectly with the landscape. I remember not being so speedy. Years later, when I was teaching at the Stevens Institute of Technology, I enjoyed crossing the river to Hoboken. In the early eighties, it still looked like the fifties! It was charming to be "outside" Manhattan, to be able to look back and wave.

In this evocative anthology, Joel Lewis has managed to cover a lot of bases in one's sense of a New Jersey poetry. The variety of experience is broad, yet contained under one banner of place, exuding an atmosphere both ordinary and magical. Three of our best poets are from New Jersey: Walt Whitman of Camden, Rutherford's William Carlos Williams, and Patersonian Allen Ginsberg. These three poets all manifest the edges of quotidian reality, the particulars of landscape, the passing human speech, and the oddities of local speech. Attention to detail, to the organics of heart and locale, to the ordinary mind of situations is pleasing in poetry and this tradition is carried on in this collection. Reading these works makes me nostalgic for the ineffable quality of my own experiences of New Jersey. Whether it be Joseph Ceravolo in a child's mind hesitating before the powerful ocean of "tin waves" trying to decide whether or not to go in, and simply noticing "The pail is near me / again. My shoulders have sand on them," or Madeline Tiger's "huge grey gull / over the Jersey Turnpike / steely as Amtrak," I experience a kind of heartbreak. Ginsberg's Aunt Rose is still "limping down the long hall in Newark" before Hitler is dead. August Kleinzahler is walking with his father in an "air full of living dust: / bus exhaust, airborne grains of pizza crust." Elizabeth Socolow's meditative car ride is rich and compassionate: "I love these men who work farms . . ." And Alfred Starr Hamilton writes the sun grows "hoarse" visiting the windowpanes of the tenements, the "new jersey iron saints." The wistfulness comes from the honesty of things as they are, or were. This book generously extends one's sense of the tenderness and beauty of being located in the specifics of place.

Anne Waldman
The Jack Kerouac School of Disembodied Poetics
The Naropa Institute
Boulder, Colorado

Preface

This poetry anthology is the fulfillment of a dream I've had for quite a while—to gather a representative sampling of the New Jersey poets so as to document the vital and diverse writing community at work in this state. That this dream has been realized is slightly astounding to me, to say the least.

If it were not for the initial interest and subsequent guidance of my editor, Leslie Mitchner, this anthology would (to paraphrase Allen Ginsberg) be published only in heaven. In a period where few editors would take a chance on publishing poetry, she responded to my project with enthusiasm and encouragement. I am grateful for that chance and for the trust she put in me by allowing me free rein on the choices I made for the poets and poems included in this volume.

A collective thank-you is due to the staff of the Rutgers University Press who participated in the realization of this anthology. But a more particularized thank-you must go to Dina Bednarczyk for her aid in making my journey through the Byzantine world of permissions and releases a little easier. Thanks also to Marilyn Campbell, Barbara Kopel, and Ann Sweeney. A special thanks is due to my copyeditor Stuart Mitchner, a fellow admirer of New Jersey's man-made landscape, for his careful reading and editing of the manuscript.

The cooperation of the poets in this book made my task as editor easier. They responded to my tight deadline with prompt delivery of material and, later, made themselves available during the preparation of the manuscript. Particular thanks are due Allen Ginsberg, David Keller, Stephen Dunn, and Alicia Suskin Ostriker.

A Jewish proverb states: "It's not good to be alone—even in Paradise." In light of that admonition, I'd like to thank the friends who offered encouragement and support while I was working on the anthology: Ibex and Emo Bumpas, Clark Coolidge, Yolanda

De Artegea, Pat Ethridge, Ed Foster, Elissa Greenwald, Gary Lenhart, and Susan Ellis Wolf. To my brother, Philip, a thank-you for the many free meals through his "Lewis Foundation for Starving Poets & Scholars."

And a very special thank-you must go to my wife, Sandy Flitterman-Lewis. Her wise and insightful advice has surely shaped this book for the better. She has been a constant source of encouragement and support in more ways than she realizes—the least of which includes sitting through endless poetry readings and enduring my Captain Beefheart and Cecil Taylor records!

Introduction

Bluestones and salt hay, two products that are indigenous to New Jersey, are found in two singular regions that give lie to the myth that this state's landscape consists only of what can be viewed from the New Jersey Turnpike. Bluestone is the popular name given to the basalt rock that is found in the New Jersey Palisades, a twelve-mile stretch of sheer cliffs that rise dramatically from the Hudson River. Although bluestone is no longer quarried in the Palisades, buildings made from it can be found throughout Hudson and Bergen counties. A good portion of lower Manhattan is made from bluestone, though, in this instance, it is the Manhattan land mass rather than its buildings. Wood cribs loaded with bluestone were used as landfill to expand the city to much of its present boundary. Thanks to the efforts of conservationists, quarrying ceased at the beginning of this century, with the upper portion of the Palisades saved from the quarrymen's dynamite caps by being made into a state park.

Salt hay is the name given to the cordgrass found in the saltwater meadows of South Jersey's vast Pine Barrens. Once harvested and processed, salt hay is put to many eminently practical purposes. In the eighteenth and nineteenth centuries, it was grazed upon by cattle and baled for winter feed, along with being used as packing material in the glassworks, pottery kilns, and brickyards that once flourished. During one period, it was pulped for use as butcher paper. Other uses include mulch, winter cover on beaches, and rope used in the casting of iron pipes. The difficult work of harvesting salt hay goes on to this day, a tribute to the genius of the residents of the Pine Barrens who, for over two hundred years, have made a life from lands once thought too "barren" for farming or permanent habitation.

Both bluestone and salt hay provide representations of the land and life in New Jersey. The very solidity of bluestone, found in the industrial northern end of the state, signifies the man-made landscape characteristic of that area. This is the New Jersey best known to the nation and it is where most of the state's population lives. Salt hay, a diminishing crop due partially to the fragile nature of the marshlands in which it is found, speaks of the largely unknown southern portion of the state—the Pine Barrens itself one of the most sparsely settled areas in the extended urban belt stretching along the Atlantic Seaboard from Boston to Washington, D.C.

The poets gathered in this anthology speak of the range and diversity of this state in their poetry. From listening posts as different as South Jersey's Port Republic and Passaic County's Paterson (founded as America's first industrial park by Alexander Hamilton), poets write of their communities, of their friends and neighbors, and of their emotions and reactions to the daily dance, in whatever form it may take or context it may find. A gathering such as this would have seemed laughable a generation ago—after all, as common wisdom would have had it, there's no culture in New Jersey. William Carlos Williams was just a fluke and, besides, what's poetic about malls and oil refineries? This book, I hope, will put to rest such silliness; after all, many of the poets contained herein are familiar names to that hardy tribe called "the readers of poetry." And for those poets unknown to the reader, he or she may be surprised at the quality of writing that has, until this publication, been an open secret known only to this state's writing community.

That so many poems in this book are about the people and landscape of the state may have to do with the changing self-perception of its residents. After years of a seemingly endless series of jokes, put-downs, and stereotypes, it appears that the long-discussed problem of New Jersey's identity crisis is on the way to something akin to a positive resolution. In the last few years, the news emanating from the Garden State isn't all of corruption, chemical factory disasters, and toxic waste dumps in residential neighborhoods. The Hackensack Meadowlands, once referred to darkly as the "Jersey Swamps," is now bearing the fruits of careful management with a mix that includes the massive Meadowlands Sports Complex, the exclusive townhouses of Harmon Cove, and Richard DeKorte State Park, the latter's masterplan calling for the restoration of the long-vanished cedar groves that William Carlos Williams recalled from his childhood in Rutherford. Economically, New Jersey is enjoying a remarkable period of prosperity marked by a diversified job market and consistently low unemployment rates; wherever one travels in the state, there seems to be another office building rising, a shopping mall under construction, or a condominium offering units for sale. Although many New Jersey cities suffer from the same ills that plague other urban centers, the successful rebirth of Hoboken has attracted national media attention and has made that city more than just a tagline to jokes that were stale even in the days of vaudeville. And, in the wake of the 1988 national political conventions that prominently featured both Governor Thomas Kean and Senator Bill Bradley, it appears that New Jersey has shaken the image of a state run by political bosses that has lingered even past the days when Jersey City Mayor Frank "I Am The Law" Hague did indeed run most of the state, voting the tombstones in the twenties and thirties to insure a continued Democratic plurality.

Though the above economic indicators have made New Jersey a more attractive proposition to business investors and potential residents, it is the arts that have helped greatly in changing how the rest of America perceives us. Bruce Springsteen of Rumson has become our unofficial good-will ambassador to the world, universalizing the experience of growing up here through his lyrics about life in small-town, working-class New Jersey. Springsteen romanticized the once-scorned highways, tract housing, and boardwalks of this state, while at same time saying "people live here!" and affirming the value and essential dignity of quiet lives away from the glimmerglass of New York City and Philadelphia, those twin dazzle palaces which many assume hold our state in thrall. Although there had been many successful bands originating from New Jersey (the Rascals, the Four Seasons, and the Vanilla Fudge among them), Bruce Springsteen was the first to make a point of emphasizing his origins. Not only did he entitle his first album *Greetings from Asbury Park* but in many of his songs you could almost smell the surf at Belmar and see head lamps rebounding off a reflector post on a pitted county road. In

Springsteen's world, the citizens of this state are given a full dimension beyond the rather cardboard-cutout stereotype of the commuter going to a Philadelphia or Manhattan job, then returning, automaton-like, to his or her "bedroom" community (as if all people did in New Jersey was sleep!).

In a smaller way, the poets of New Jersey have shared Springsteen's commitment to uncovering the "real" in the daily life that surrounds them. "Poetry is life distilled," said Gwendolyn Brooks, and the poets of this state have collectively been documenting life here in New Jersey better than any newspaper or TV newscast. Ezra Pound defined poetry's content as news that stays new and that definition is the secret power of the poet. The good poem combines information and an emotional investment in that information. It can focus on what others may consider trivial and thus provide a document for future readers of what people felt at a particular time, rather than the thin-air of statistics and graphs. Just as we might read the Brownings or Tennyson to understand the Victorian mind, or read Walt Whitman for his poetic reportage of the Civil War years, it is quite possible that future cultural historians might use a collection such as this to gauge the social weather of a particular place in a particular time.

And just who are these poets, anyway? Unlike the artist or musician, there is no real social space for the poet other than the printed page. True, the institution of the poetry reading is long-established in New Jersey; yet, in most instances, readings are vector points where poets can meet one another and exchange ideas and present earlier versions of texts that may live on the page of a magazine or, better yet, a book. Poets find themselves somewhere in the realm between artisan and artist; we talk of the "art" of the novel—yet poetry is referred to as a "craft," more and more perfected these days in the writing workshop (compared to the musician's conservatory and the ballet's academy). And in contemporary society, the poet's audience is often fellow poets. Although some blame this happenstance on the swerve into complexity that poetry made with the advent of modernism (as if William Wordsworth and Robert Browning were "easy reads"), I think there are too many mitigating factors—including the creation of the new mediums of the cinema, radio, and television, the breakthrough fictions of James Joyce and Virginia Woolf, and the loss of a common set of cultural referents needed for a mass poetry—to fix blame on a particular group or event. Despite grim forecasts, poetry continues on, perhaps not at the forefront of the arts, but with enough presence for it to remain a kind of *jouissance* for the other arts, as in such phrases as "a poetic film," "a lyrical painting," or in referring to literate song lyrics such as those by Bob Dylan and Joni Mitchell as "poetry." Perhaps the attraction of the poetic is in its intrinsic opposition to the daily economic world of commerce and business, existing, as the critic Barbara Johnson has noted, as the surplus value of daily language. Poetry, with its small but fiercely loyal audience, represents a principle of hope to those caught in its spell, a small utopia for some of our daylight dreams.

This all being said in making the case for poets and poetry, it might come as a bit of a letdown to the reader to learn that poets of New Jersey prefer the company of men and women to Parnassus. There is no profile that easily fits our poets. Some teach in our colleges and secondary schools. Others work as poets-in-residence with the state-sponsored Poets-in-the Schools (PITS) program or the private Geraldine R. Dodge Foundation. Among the poets in this book, the job description can range from retired candy-store owner to computer programmer. The New Jersey poet can be your co-worker, a fellow PTA member or (if he or she holds to the traditions of poetry) a clerk in the local bookstore.

Though there is no real center for poetic activity in New Jersey, when poets find one another in any part of the state, a community is born. Poetry readings are held at colleges, state parks, historic houses, and the backrooms of bars. Magazines publish the works of local and national writers, the formats ranging from photocopied, side-stapled, one-shot efforts to well-bound quarterlies published on quality bond. Small presses exist, too, as do poetry programs on radio. In fact, the quality and variety of the New Jersey community of poets makes it one of the most active and vital centers for American poetry.

Historically, the poets of New Jersey have always been a presence in American literature. Philip Freneau (1752–1832), generally considered to be the first American poet of note, lived most of his life at Mount Pleasant, his family's home near Middletown Point. Best known for political verse written in the cause of the American Revolution, Freneau also wrote "The Indian Burying Ground," the first poem by an American using an Indian theme, along with "The Wild Honeysuckle," which was once called "the first stammer of nature poetry in America." It is worth noting that Freneau wrote in a workmanlike diction appropriate to his calling as a "plain-dealing republican bard." Although ignored and sometimes reviled by his contemporaries as nothing more than a propagandist or "newspaper" poet, he remains one of the few poets of his period, save for Phillis Wheatley, who is read today.

New Jersey was the site of much literary activity in the earlier years of the Republic. Washington Irving (1783–1859), though associated with the Hudson Valley of upstate New York, began his serious literary career in Newark in 1806–1807. His participation in the wild parties held at that city's Cockloft Hall inspired the satiric *Salmagundi* papers, his first literary success. During this period he wrote poetry describing the Passaic River and its environs. William Cullen Bryant, a member of Irving's Knickerbocker circle, lived in Hoboken from 1832 to 1834, along with being a frequent visitor from the late 1820s to the late 1840s. Hoboken, hard as may be to believe, was once a bucolic parkland frequented by New Yorkers in the years before the creation of Central Park. Though little of Bryant's nature poetry is sitespecific, one poem ("Noon") situates the poem's speaker on a "brow of rock / That overlooks the Hudson's western marge"—that is, Weehawken's Palisades. In those early romantic days of the Republic, many of Bryant's Knickerbocker friends took the ferry across the Hudson to walk the tree-lined River Walk (now the very functional Frank Sinatra Drive), imbibe at Sybil's Cave, and write witty verse while spending an afternoon at Elysian Fields (now a coffee factory).

After the Knickerbocker group departed from Hoboken in the 1830s, New Jersey experienced a shortage of first-rank poets. In the days before grants and teaching appointments, the serious writer sought his or her fame in New York, Boston, and Philadelphia. As Larzer Ziff noted in his study *Literary Democracy*, the early years of the nation were marked by a great interest in a national literature, with the leading literary journals achieving a circulation of over forty thousand—this at a time when most of the country was illiterate. The young writer could find work writing for these journals and stand a better chance of being discovered than he would in the wilds of Jersey. Although poets of the era practiced their craft here, nothing of this period survived the generation in which it was written.

In 1873 a partially paralyzed poet came to Camden to recover his health at his brother's house. Although the best of Walt Whitman's poetry was behind him, it was in Camden that he became the "Good Gray Poet" admirers came to visit. Beyond his age and frail health, it was a far different Whitman who came to live in Camden than the virile figure staring back to the few readers of the initial 1855 printing of *Leaves of Grass*. During his years in Camden, where he listed himself in the city directory as "Whitman, Walt, Poet," he was able to live on publishing royalties and lecture fees and, by 1884, had saved enough to purchase a small home on Mickle Street that exists today as a historic site and a shrine to that most American of poets.

Whitman wrote little that directly refers to Camden, given the cosmic concerns of his poetry. He was a familiar sight in the city, however, walking its streets and engaging his fellow citizens in conversation. According to the *WPA Guide to 1930s New Jersey* (Rutgers University Press reissue), Whitman preferred to converse with children and workers, and could occasionally be found in a local tavern having "a short drink—or champagne on gala days—and a long talk." The image of the gentle, fatherly Whitman that we know today is formed from the numerous accounts of the poet during his last two decades in Camden, most notably Horace Truabel's multivolume *With Walt Whitman in Camden*. Besides being Whitman's Boswell, Traubel (1858–1919) was a Camden native, a socialist activist, and one of the first Jewish-American poets. Though his poetry is forgotten nowadays, his *Chants Democratic* and *Chants American* are interesting volumes that explore the poetic ground Whitman opened for future generations of writers.

Stephen Crane (1871–1900), while best known for his novels and short stories, left behind a body of poetry considered to be a precursor to American modernism. Born on 14 Mulberry Street in Newark, Crane spent his teens in Asbury Park, where he first broke into print with some unsigned newspaper articles for a column called "On the New Jersey Coast." His two volumes of poetry, *Black Riders* and *War Is Kind*, share with the poetry of Herman Melville a realism that stands out from the Victorian artifice that was endemic to the poetry of their time. After the poet's death in Europe, his body was returned for burial in Hillside, near Newark.

Although his name has become synonymous with popular sentimental verse, it should be remembered that Joyce Kilmer (1886–1918) was a reflection of that last generation before movies, radio, and TV for whom reading was a main leisure activity. Kilmer was only one of many popular poets of his day whose name was familiar to the general public. A convert to Catholicism who also invented an Irish identity, Kilmer's inspiration for his most famous poem came to him while waiting for a train to Hoboken at Mahwah's Erie Railroad station. First published in *Poetry* in 1913 and then a year later as the title poem of Kilmer's first book, "Trees" was set to music, sung upon the vaudeville stage, and burned forever into the minds of millions of American schoolchildren (usually in the course of an Arbor Day program). Kilmer, who supported himself as a literary journalist, edited *Dreams and Images: An Anthology of Catholic Poets*—a serious and groundbreaking work that was in print for many years.

The career of the Rutherford poet-physician William Carlos Williams (1883–1963) is testimony to the fact that one can live in "provincial" suburban New Jersey and still make great art. Though his good friend Ezra Pound told him that Rutherford was no place to write poetry, Williams stayed and, eventually, prospered. Certainly, though, the road was not easy. He had to subsidize the publication of his early books and then was not published by a major press (Random House) until he was almost seventy—in contrast to friends and peers such as Marianne Moore, e. e. cummings, and Wallace Stevens, who enjoyed the prestige and power of being on the list of a commercial publisher. In his home state, poets such as Amelia Josephine Barr, Mrs. Dwight W. Morrow (mother of Anne Morrow Lindbergh), Louis Ginsberg (father of Allen Ginsberg), and Leonard H. Robbins (author of the singular *Jersey Jingles*) represented the "official" poetry of the period.

Williams continued writing, despite the prospect of continued obscurity, as if banking on the eventuality of an audience that could understand his quotidian experiments in the American measure. Fame did come to him, albeit slowly and in incremental steps. A generation of poets—Robert Creeley, Robert Lowell, Denise Levertov, and Charles Olson among them—visited his house on 9 Ridge Road both to pay homage and to learn from the doctor. Williams's influence became so pervasive in American poetry that the contemporary neo-Formalist movement sees itself as the David hurling iambs against a Goliath manifested in the form of Dr. Williams's poetic children—a near total reversal of the situation that existed in American poetry at the time of his death. Williams goes beyond being merely a stylistic guide for the poets of New Jersey: he serves as something of a permission-giver. Williams junked the great romantic mantle that poetry had attached itself to—poetry was not merely a recording of the sublime but of imaginative transformations of everyday events.

Four years after Williams's death, the first fellowships of the year-old New Jersey State Council on the Arts (NJSCA) were awarded to artists of the various disciplines, including poets. And a few years after the creation of the NJSCA, the antiwar movement helped launch a public awareness of poetry that exceeded the previous decade's interest in the Beats. As those who lived through that era might remember, no rally or demonstration was complete without the participation of a poet or poets. The movement mimeo machine often did double duty for the local literary magazine. And poets such as Robert Lowell, Denise Levertov, and W. S. Merwin, who were outspoken in their opposition to the war, became cultural heroes to a generation.

In New Jersey, the rhizomes that eventually create a community began appearing throughout the state. In New Brunswick, the Brecht West series attracted many from the Rutgers University community. Regular readings were also held at the campuses of Princeton and Seton Hall. In Hudson County, John Ensslin put on readings in venues ranging from a local art gallery to an old firehouse. In the spring of 1969, the Bergen Poets began a series of workshops through which many poets of that area began their writing careers. In 1973, the US 1 Poets Cooperative began to hold workshops and readings around the Princeton area, eventually becoming one of the must successful groups of its kind in the country.

It was during the "Me Generation" seventies that the New Jersey poetry community coalesced. The state-sponsored PITS program and a similar program run by the Dodge Foundation offered the chance to make a living as a poet. Local colleges, taking a cue from the national trend, began hiring poets-in-residence onto their faculties in greater numbers. Funded by CETA grants, local writing projects held workshops that helped develop area writers. Group readings, such as those held by *Lunch* magazine at Fairleigh Dickinson University's Rutherford campus, would attract hundreds to events that often went on until the early morning. The William Carlos Williams Poetry Festival, held near the Great Falls of Paterson Williams immortalized, became a media event that made the general public aware that there were poets among them. The poetry community currently active in the state is, to a great extent, a continuum of the activities of the last twenty years.

The poems and poets selected for inclusion in this anthology represent a cross-section of the most interesting work going on in the state, from Alfred Starr Hamilton, one of the last writers of folk poetry, to the formalism of Theodore Weiss. Contemporary anthologies too often distort the range of American poetry by weighing the selections toward one school, then proclaiming the work collected as being "representative" of a region, generation, or, worse, a nation. This volume is by no means to be taken as the definitive collection of this state's poets, as if such a creature exists. Like all anthologists faced with the task of boiling down a small mountain of manuscripts to a representative selection, I depend more on my own taste and judgment than the sometimes misleading prejudgment of awards and lengthy vitae. Although many anthologists regret that space limitations keep them from including all the poets deserving inclusion, I have come to the conclusion that such limits (to paraphrase Samuel Johnson's comments on executions) make one's mind focus wonderfully on the task at hand.

Another aspect of the editing of this volume was an attempt to create an anthology *about* New Jersey, instead of an anthology of poets who merely happen to pay taxes to the same state authority. The reader will find a number of poems addressed to Walt Whitman written by poets of quite different aesthetic stances. The William Carlos Williams tradition can be seen in the work of both Edward R. Smith and August Kleinzahler. Allen Ginsberg, whose two early books were prefaced by Williams, is of course a poet of great influence—traceries here found in the work of Herschel Silverman and Eliot Katz. Alicia Ostriker, a mentor to a generation of poets who have attended Rutgers University, is represented here by her wonderfully precise and insightful poems on New Jersey life.

Those who are only acquainted with Allen Ginsberg's *Howl* and *Kaddish*, may find the gentle lyricism of his New Jersey poems something of a surprise. For those of us who have followed the poet's journey of almost four decades, these works represent one aspect of a distinguished career. In "Garden State," which was first published in 1980 in my own *Ahnoi* magazine, he offers advice to the poets of this state: "Look for the News in your own backyard / over the whitewashed picket fence, fading signs / on upper stories of red brick factories." And for a poet perceived as being so at odds with normative values of the square world, poems like the sequence to his father and "To Aunt Rose" display a tenderness and compassion rarely seen in recent American verse.

A number of poets included in this volume came to my attention through the suggestion of my colleagues. David Keller's work was a wonderful find for me, his poetry displaying a human voice at work without the sort of artifice that one seems to encounter so often in contemporary writing. Two poets directed me to the work of Elizabeth Socolow, and I was pleased that these recommendations were fully justified. Through one poet's urging, I set out to contact Sean T. Farragher—a poet who seemed to have dropped from sight in the last few years. I had almost given up when I opened a paper to an article on Farragher that noted both his return to publishing and his current residence. The results of my investigations are contained herein.

The preponderance of a New Jersey thematic in these poems makes this book like a literary town meeting with the poets as neighbors talking across fences, formica dinner tables, train aisles, and workbenches about their friends, families, and hometowns. That talk can range from the political hardball of Amiri Baraka to Jim Handlin's introspective meditations. Despite the ascribed difficulty of understanding contemporary poetry, poets really do want to be understood by their readers—and a tradition of Jersey plain-speaking that starts with Freneau lives on in many of these poems. Charles Olson said in the *Maximus Poems* "that we are only as we find out we are," a pithy description of the poetic process at work throughout *Bluestones and Salt Hay*. Any good poem, any good work of art, must have in it some degree of discovery and surprise or what results is often an exercise in style that reveals a lack of emotional investment from its author. Sometimes, as Frank O'Hara once said, you just go on your nerve.

This volume of poetry from New Jersey contains an immanent argument about the value of the quotidian for poetry. Too often, poets are content to be oblivious to their own communities, refusing the landscape that presents itself daily for use. And without a sense of community, we are fated to become poets of the TV age: anonymous producers of generic texts. Too often, the contemporary poem is near white-writing—ahistoric, lacking place, and revealing the cookie-cutter traces of the style of the particular writing program from which it has descended.

In a period in which our traditional concepts of neighborhood and community have been severely revised, the question becomes "How does the poet fit into his or her topography?" It's no secret to the practicing poet that his/her craft is the most marginal of the disciplines and that situation in New Jersey is not much different than in most places in America. However, what distinguishes New Jersey from other regions in the nation is the literary inheritance that writers can draw upon. This tradition is particularly focused upon that still-felt presence of the Rutherford doctor, William Carlos Williams, who once said, "I want to use the words we speak and to describe the things we see, as far as it can be done." From his short lyrics of the thirties to his book-length *Paterson*, Williams's oeuvre affirms the fact that one's everyday landscape can be the proper subject for a poem. This notion that one's life and experience could be the basis for poetic production ultimately created the basis for American poetry as we know it today.

However, and despite Dr. Williams's vast shade, a new measure must be created for this generation and its particular version of New Jersey. In this volume we can see the groundwork for that task. So many voices. And so many methods at work in recreating daily life in imaginative language. Perhaps for poetry to again become relevant to the general literary community, it may have to go backwards to reclaim its social function. The poet was once the community's historian, its public conscience, the mythmaker and the celebrator of great events. That contemporary poetry's potential readers may prefer the critical writings of Jacques Derrida (itself a new kind of literature) or the novels of Don DeLillo has something to do with the fact that the reader can find more of the *real* in those texts than in most poems they happen to encounter. The work contained in *Bluestones and Salt Hay* offers an alternative to that totemic generic poem because these poets speak to their readers in the same passionate and direct way New Jersey poets have been doing since the days of Freneau.

The drama of poetry is that it exists in a continual state of emergency as opposed to the dead language its critics have made it out to be. At bottom, according to Paul Valery, poets have no social obligations, save to leave their native language a little richer than it was before. But to escape the trap of what Jack Spicer called the "Big Lie of the Personal"—that poem which offers a series of sensory images claiming to encode universal human emotions—we have to return to the world outside ourselves, as well as the landscape of language. A non-negotiable demand for poets should be: always the active voice, and to use history and not be used by it.

As I put the final touches on this introduction, I can smell the pungent arabica beans roasting in the ovens of Hoboken's waterfront Maxwell House Coffee factory—"Mile Square City's" last major factory, built upon the site of the first organized baseball game. The street life on Washington Street is mostly teenagers eating pizza on blue slate stoops, with the occasional commuter sauntering up from the PATH trains. On some nights, the magic is just right—a rattling fan is music and the moon is a bright drip on a dark car's hood. And I'm sure the magic was there when the late earthworks artist Robert Smithson wrote this description of his hometown, Clifton, in his essay "The Crystal Land": "Most of the houses are painted white, but many are painted petal pink, frosted mint, buttercup, fudge, rose beige, antique green, Cape Cod brown, lilac and so on. The highways crisscross through the towns and become man-made geological networks of concrete. In fact, the entire landscape has a mineral presence. From the shiny chrome diners to glass windows of shopping centers, a sense of the crystalline prevails."

Joel Lewis
Hoboken, N.J.

Bluestones and Salt Hay

AMIRI BARAKA

In Memory of Radio

Who has ever stopped to think of the divinity of Lamont
    Cranston?
(Only Jack Kerouac, that I know of: & me.
The rest of you probably had on WCBS and Kate Smith.
Or something equally unattractive.)

What can I say?
It is better to have loved and lost
Than to put linoleum in your living rooms?

Am I a sage or something?
Mandrake's hypnotic gesture of the week?
(Remember, I do not have the healing powers of Oral
    Roberts . . .
I cannot, like F. J. Sheen, tell you how to get saved & *rich!*
I cannot even order you to gaschamber satori like Hitler or
    Goody Knight

& Love is an evil word.
Turn it backwards/see, see what I mean?
An evol word, & besides
who understands it?
I certainly wouldn't like to go out on that kind of limb.

Saturday mornings we listened to *Red Lantern* & his
    undersea folk.
At 11, *Let's Pretend*/& we did/& I, the poet, still do.
    Thank God!

What was it he used to say (after the transformation, when he
    was safe
& invisible & the unbelievers couldn't throw stones?)
    "Heh, heh, heh,
Who knows what evil lurks in the hearts of men? The
    Shadow knows."

O, yes he does
O, yes he does.
An evil word it is,
This Love.

Cops

flyolfloyd, i know from barringer,
he used to be the daredevil sax playing
lover of the old sod, near the hip park
where they threw you in, he, with some others,
notably Allen Polite, was a lover, and smooth as anything
    blowin
in them parts, in that town, in that time
he weighs 400 now
and threatens junkies
on Howard Street, calling them by first or nick
names, really scaring the piss out of them, being
"a nice guy" and all his killings being accidental.
Bowleg Otis played football but was always a prick
he made detective by arresting a dude he knew all his life,
he waited in the cold counting white folks' smiles. Lenny
drives a panel truck, Leon parkd in front of the city hospital
bullshitting, but he'd split yr head. He was a bad catchr w/
Baxter Terrace, you slide home head first you get messed up
strong as a bitch. Hubert Friday, beat up Barry one night,
Hubie was a funnytime cat never played anything. Cats used to

pop his sister. You wanna stand in front of a bar, with a gun
pointed at you? You wanna try to remember why you liked
    somebody
while the bullet comes. Shit.

Against Bourgeois Art

War on the horizon. a ship with bloody sail. Andy Young slips
    on his
Chamberlain appeasement getup he got from years listening to
    the cp
hype martin luther king. Is there somebody here to record this?
    US being
thrown out the front door, the Russian bear charging through
    the back door.
Carmichael suddenly clearly an apologist for newstyle
    colonialism.
Telling us we cant fight in the US. Though centuries of our
    dead are buried
here. Oceans of our blood have fertilized a black nation
    (Afri-zone) in the south. Is
there someone, here, to get this down? Can I get a, like they
    say, witness.
An eye that can see through this here. In Jimmy Carters Snake
    Oil Show there
is a room nobody talks about. Steel door, fumes seep
    underneath. Inside,
blood and hair on the floor, bones stacked in the corner. Photos
    of Goering,
Goebbels, Joe McCarthy and Nixon in the nude trying to put
    helmets on their
pecker wooed. Will somebody put this stuff out, you walk thru a
    museum all

the colors of the spectrum right there but not one image, except of checks
passing, Pollockdollarsigns, Dekooning fortunes, Larry Rivers pots at the
end of the rain bow
no people
no love
no heart and soul insides flowing out
no fighting in the street
no fires rip the sky
no children screaming death
no police
no state, except it is the state, bullshitting
on the wall
no people struggle, just colors thrown by baby snooks
a down and leaving unintellectual
no record of this place.
As wild a motherfucking joint as america is
somebody shd get this shit down, otherwise no one will believe it.
Get it down
Get it on the record
Get the hate the horror the lies the Rockefeller Monsters
eating corpses
Hey, bro, say, hey, what it is, dude, yeh, too too, do it is ya?
wow low, dootie roo, bay bay bay beeeeeee. carrying a radio on his soulda
eating corpses
coal mines
garment center
assembly lines
hot steaming steel poured through space
not any of life is there
hey poet, you artist
he turns in the shadows sucking a marble, dribbling andy warhol's lost nut
he is an artist

he is a po eight
a po nine too
his work is about everything
his work is about the universe
her work is about stars belching
her work is about grey hair lost in the desert peeped in a teeny
    voice
no babies
no screams
no red life
no future
death peeped in a teeny voice,
stupidity dripped in a sultry voice
bourgeois poets yodel nonsense about boring absence
they think up funny ways for letters to sit on the page
concrete bullshit, arty dumbshit, they are safe as old toilet paper
Revolution sweeps the world, Bourgeois artists stare at crumbs
    of dust in the light
People change reality. But these dull imitation poets talk to us
    of fragmented
nothingness. Like two-celled creatures trying to bebop, the
    world is heavier
than they know. They do not know. They fight knowledge with
    abstraction and
think they cool because they talk to they self. They are full of
    shit
like vultures "pecking" on an open grave
They uphold dying capitalism and give themselves airs
They think they shit is profound, and complex
But the people think its as profound and complex as monkey
    farts
Now meditate
on that!

Cold Term

All the things. The objects.
Cold freeze of the park, while
passing. People there. White inside
outside on horses trotting ignorantly
There is so much pain for our blackness
so much beauty there, if we think to what
our beautiful selves would make
of the world, steaming turning blackouts
over cold georgia, the spirits hover
waiting for the world to arrive at ecstasy.
Why cant we love each other and be beautiful?
Why do the beautiful corner each other and spit
poison? Why do the beautiful not hangout together
and learn to do away with evil? Why are the beautiful
not living together and feeling each other's trials?
Why are the beautiful not walking with their arms around
each other laughing softly at the soft laughter of black beauty?
Why are the beautiful dreading each other, and hiding from
each other? Why are the beautiful sick and divided
like myself?

Money

Prophets
become
Profits
reveals
Religion
give way

                              to
Capitalism

Obscene Rich Motherfuckers
Who fuck up the
                    world
              For *Money*

Who took slaves and enslaved
                    Africa
              For *Money*
they have no God
              But Money

Education is to make money
Books & Cars made 1st for
              Money
              No book publishing
              or movie making

              except for money.

They have Killed
              & lied & raped
              & repressed
              enslaved
              &
              butchered

  disinfor
              mated
                    & had niggers castrated
                    for money
                    Lynched
                    & Destroyed
                      opposed
                      beauty

&
evolution
focus
of a
revolution
for Money.

they threaten to kill us
everything
for money

they fuck up the water, kill
fish and birds.
radioactively annihilate
public & secret
millions

for Money
They have no God no perceived
Good
But Money

Sin is
Poverty
Outsiders
Creativity
Not from
Europe

No God Nothing
they wd live
or die for
but Money

Remember the Ojays
when they 1st was sure
sd it was Money
Lowell Fuller , James Brown

Jesus said it was
impossible
for a rich man
to be good
No camels pass
            thru
        no needles'
        eyes
why God and the prophets
of the ancient world
            Condemned the worship
        of *Baal*
The Golden Calf
            Animalism
            Glorified

The perfection of this
            world
            is the
        purpose of life
            naturally
in twain to define
            Consciousness
Change & Develop
        as creators
        and creations
        of what is
        Living
        Knowing
        (The Dead
In his own image
            its
        own
        as Good itself
in all accents.

10.88

Amiri Baraka   9

ALLIFESTO*!*

Oleo (Miles)

As Swingingest
is
Peace
&
Wisdom

as Funk is the
Soul's
smell
as
it
creates

As Heat is
Spirit
Breathing
Rhythm
God's
only
Life

in us beats
is
against
aint

That life is the creation
of Jass
& so lo
is the Sun
coming
out

His Mama
whole

so then
HOLY
DIGGER
WRETCHED
NIGGER

Charlie Parker meant Soul
even to the Ancient
Egyptians
Monk
was
Title
you got
When you come out the
Mystery
School
Thot
always
rode in a

Trane
Gold
Energy
Traveler

Reigning
& Raining
& Reining

on everything
living

Rays
Gods
Kings

Science
Civilization
Art

Therefore
Always Be
Conscious
&
Hip too!

BeBop is
holier
than
Capitalism!

&
Blue has
Always
been
our
favorite
color!

10/88
Year of the Mardi Gras

KENNETH BURKE

And Here I Am, Fighting Dandelions

It's not their bright yellow
more frank than boastful.

Yet, though hurried and harried
careering and careening
I fare forth
to cut down dandelions.

I patrol the lawn, resenting how they spread like a foreign
policy.

At times I catch one *in flagrante delicto*
(in fragrant delight?)
in an orgy of miscegenation with a bee,
without benefit of clergy.

I dig up dandelions
at the height of their excesses.

(I fight fair.
No chemicals.
I'm a Rachel Carson man
and Organic Gardening—
and damn the fluoridation racket.)

Word goes forth:
"Burke's after us.
Hurry, proliferate,
be a population explosion."

From away back
the nice old lady next door
friendly to all
yet hypnotized by the *mores*

She raged against the Eyetalians
who swept across the grass in springtime
harvesting the honest dandelion

She fumed because they dug holes in her lawn—
or was she but responding
to the way they crouched at their work
(stoop labor)
and hurried like stage criminals,
disappearing around the corner of Friendship Avenue?

The Wrens

The wrens are back!

Their liquid song, pouring across the lawn—
(Or, if the sunlight pours, the wren's song glitters)
Up from the porch,
                        Into the bedroom, where
It is the play of light across a pond,
Sounding as small waves look: new copper coins
Between the seer and the sun.

                        Herewith
Is made a contract binding the brightly waked
Sleeper and his wren, neither the wren's
Nor his, but differently owned by both.

Behind the giving-forth, wren history;
Man-history behind the taking-in.

(Mark the city as a place where no
Wrens sing, as though April were seas of sand,
With spring not the burial of lilac,
            but heat quaking above stone.)

                        After magnetic storms
Had made all men uneasy, but those the most
That feared the loss of salary or love,

The wrens are back!

Temporary Wellbeing

The pond is plenteous
The land is lush,
And having turned off the news
I am for the moment mellow.

With my book in one hand
And my drink in the other
What more could I want

But fame,
Better health,
And ten million dollars?

Trick Weather

Snow-bearing wind
Among dried leaves
On oak saplings

Sizzles like spring rain
This February late afternoon.

Soon leaves fall, scatter
In March wind.

Oak leaves blowing in March
Sure sign of spring

Part of a Letter

Remember that night, after the card game
We went bumping down the road
drunk
insulting each other.

You said things so vicious
the next day you apologized.

But I could not recall a one of them.
I was robbed.

Yours for that most momentous of words: "Vindication"—
it is the labyrinthine word.
All hail to Mighty Æschylus.

Beat the devil, beat the devil, beat the devil,
Beat the devil, beat the devil, beat the . . .

(Hear the train
Drive steadily on
Towards nowhere)

Interlude

"Who are you?"
  The sweet girl asked,
  Her face twistedly bepuzzled.

I should say the truth, I don't know?
Or, in terms of insecurity,
"008—22—8559"?
Or my phone number:
Two billion,
Thirteen million,
Four hundred and seventy-three thousand,
Two hundred and forty-nine?

I gave the literal name—
And, passing, she repeated it.

Then, bethinking me, I turned and shouted after,
"But who are *you?*"
  She called back,
"I'm Heidi."

Heidi, Heidi, Heidi,
Name-magic from out my childhood,
Mine Schweitzer Alpine Heidi,
And all this time a-hiding.

Name from the first of books
I ever loving heard,
In whatever of impermanence and changelessness
I have prayed, "God, drop me quick down dead,
If only others are not thus in jeopardy,"
The little girl called back,
"I'm Heidi."

As From a Greek Anthology

Do the violets, like me, tug at their roots this warm day of
   late autumn?
Already I can imagine late April, yet we have not even had
   our first snow-flurry.
When I was young, spring came upon me suddenly, with me
   still thinking of the pleasures of the sleigh.
But if I expect it always earlier and earlier
I shall soon overtake it by a cycle,
And be expecting spring in the springtime.

Buildings Should Not Be Tall

Buildings should not be tall, that we be spared
The need to walk in gulches. Of their pride
We are the squalor. We the traffick-eyed,
Stench-nostriled, Klaxon-eared and thinning-haired,
Inhabiting a city's underside,
By this man-made biology prepared
To cower in meekness, hurried and beglared,
And somehow live until we've somehow died.

These are our masters, basking in the sun—
It is our owners that we crawl among.
In such granitic utterance they reveal
Self-portraitures of greed that rose up, when
A grasping brood expressed in stone and steel
Its detestation of its fellow-men.

Heavy, Heavy—What Hangs Over?

At eighty
reading lines
he wrote at twenty

The storm now past

A gust in the big tree
splatters raindrops
on the roof

JOSEPH CERAVOLO

The Wind Is Blowing West

1

I am trying to decide to go swimming,
But the sea looks so calm.
All the other boys have gone in.
I can't decide what to do.

I've been waiting in my tent
Expecting to go in.
Have you forgotten to come down?
Can I escape going in?
I was just coming

I was just going in
But lost my pail

2

A boisterous tide is coming up;
I was just looking at it.
The pail is near me
again. My shoulders have sand on them.

Round the edge of the tide
Is the shore. The shore
Is filled with waves.
They are tin waves.

Boisterous tide coming up.
The tide is getting less.

3

Daytime is not a brain,
Living is not a cricket's song.
Why does light diffuse
As earth turns away from the sun?

I want to give my food
To a stranger. I want
to be taken.
What kind of a face do

I have while leaving?
I'm thinking of my friend.

4

I am trying to go swimming
But the sea looks so calm
All boys are gone
I can't decide what to do

I've been waiting to go
Have you come down?
Can I escape

I am just coming
        Just going in

A Railway Stop

(ORANGE, N.J.)

Two students kiss goodbye.
He boards the train laughing.
She disappears down the stairs,

disappears into the night.
It comes soon enough
against the spread-apart clouds,
or one penis smokestack
in this old industrial valley.
The hills are not high
but they surround the houses
that face the empty desolate industries.
Morning mixes into night.
The world of sorrows begins to part.

Night Birds

While the animals rest
do we have the right to divine life?
Branch Brook pond is clear.
It is a clear impossible alone.
All inner feelings are grown up
and us, two people
approaching the clear pond
with fish we see, near the edge.
It's like a vision
of the pond
but there are two children
and a man.
Is it through the pond
or the flowers around
or our talking
or the whispering of late
erotic birds?
Yes, maybe they are far
from their family.
Maybe that's why they're late

or are they just night birds
come here like they do
every night, like we do.

Meadowlands

Only a few song birds are out
they sing . . . . . . the wind brushes the grasses.
The winds brush from a golden
to a shadow of gold
over the enormous flooded.
Only the signal of a moth
only a few song birds

only the wind mixed with salt:
only the stars

Park Thoughts

O clouds above these trees
    like trees detached from trunks

It hasn't rained
nor do the genitals reign
            as they used to.

O cloud trees
                over the trees of the west
    moved to the northern sky.

Sail with the south wind
   along the coast
  toward the grotto
of our secret.

O, what bullshit!
Ah, What solitude!

Rte. 3 into N.Y.

7:53, 36 degrees
slight haze in north
very white in the east
yellow in the south
blue in the west
overhead, my mind hangs
in the transparent sky.
A bible freak next to me
 is reading, "will they
ever find Noah's Ark?"
Who cares
whether they find it or not.
Will I ever find a job?
I really do feel
like wandering off forever
and stop looking for anything
    while the wind
    carries away the smoke
    from Hoffman LaRoche
     Pharmaceuticals.

Rifle Shot

What you can't have is what
you can't have
is what you want
when you cannot want
because good times and good love
fly out of you
quicker than an automatic gun
quicker than an automatic
quicker than a gun
quicker than a particle
flies from you when you're dead.

Dream stuff, dream towns, dream schemes
act upon the heart
and wait and dream,
till all's gone, all's dissolved,
by crystal dust in space,
quicker than a spirit
when you're dead
quicker than a spirit leaves
the beauty of your face.

Winter

Ask the sun why today
a glow passes over your face
and the ice stretches in the bay
over the cool whiteness of your race.

February winds, late winter warmth
far away ancestral eyes blind
by deserts, and tundras growth
that eats up whatever I find.

Ask the sun why the day
flows over every last trace
of struggle in the sacred decay
of love in the human race.

Still Life

O hydrant, how strange it is
to be mortal flesh and blood
and die off, and be born
and be more movable than a tree
be gravity fed like all creatures
and sun fed

when at any moment
a volcano erupts poison gas,
an earth movement swallows itself
while cicadas rub sound off
in the sunny stillness,

and fool the continuity of love.

CHERYL CLARKE

Of Althea and Flaxie

In 1943 Althea was a welder
very dark
very butch
and very proud
loved to cook, sew, and drive a car
and did not care who knew she kept company with a woman
who met her every day after work
in a tight dress and high heels
light-skinned and high-cheekboned
who loved to shoot, fish, play poker
and did not give a damn who knew her 'man' was a woman.

Althea was gay and strong in 1945
and could sing a good song
from underneath her welder's mask
and did not care who heard her sing her song to a woman.

Flaxie was careful and faithful
mindful of her Southern upbringing
watchful of her tutored grace
long as they treated her like a lady
she did not give a damn who called her a 'bulldagger.'

In 1950 Althea wore suits and ties
Flaxie's favorite colors were pink and blue
People openly challenged their flamboyance
but neither cared a fig who thought them 'queer' or 'funny.'

When the girls bragged over break of their sundry loves,
Flaxie blithely told them her old lady Althea took her dancing
every weekend
and did not give a damn who knew she clung to a woman.

When the boys on her shift complained of their wives,
Althea boasted of how smart her 'stuff' Flaxie was
and did not care who knew she loved the mind of a woman.

In 1955 when Flaxie got pregnant
and Althea lost her job
Flaxie got herself on relief
and did not care how many caseworkers
threatened midnite raids.

Althea was set up and went to jail
for writing numbers in 1958.
Flaxie visited her every week with gifts
and hungered openly for her thru the bars
and did not give a damn who knew she waited for a woman.

When her mother died in 1965 in New Orleans
Flaxie demanded that Althea walk beside her in the funeral
    procession
and did not care how many aunts and uncles knew she slept
    with a woman.

When she died in 1970
Flaxie fought Althea's proper family not to have her laid out
    in lace
and dressed the body herself
and did not care who knew she'd made her way with a woman.

jazz poem for Morristown, N.J.

i pass so many dead things in the road
and grind my teeth in ecstasy
of contact
neck   middle   head
wild timid now dead
exquisite fuchsia expectorate
of entrail and brain
things
in the road.

curious . . . so many seeming sleeping
struck squash
dead decomposing
hash pink mush gray
gut exposing
things SMASH!
in the road.

strutting crows like penguins
picking a flattened rabbit
on a curve in Piscataway, New Jersey
risking dying scattering at the whine
of my startled tread
returning to pick the carcass more.
diligent buzzards striating and peeling
back neat the skin of a doe
brought down by a pickup truck
and dragged to the shoulder of an Arizona road.

in Brooklyn
children laugh at sling shot
pigeon
inside out under car wheel dead.

sad . . . so many dead things in the road.
no powers of discernment
no antennas to cross the road
to the other side
in predatory industrial encroachment
not even Lenapes* in the wood
could have saved
so many things struck dead in the road.

intestine smeared medians of whole raccoon families.

vitriolic skunk dismembered.

decapitated cowardly possum.

*Native Americans who inhabited parts of what are now known as
New Jersey.

Bulletin

Disguising her vigilance with passive
stance, she read the bulletin stealthily
with some difficulty and great understanding:

'The General will esteem it as a singular
favor if you can apprehend a mulatto girl,
servant and slave of Mrs. Washington, who
eloped from this place yesterday. She may
intend to the enemy. . . . Her name is
Charlotte but in all probability will
change it. . . . She is light-complected,
about 13 years of age, pert, and dressed
in brown cloth westcoat and petticoat. Your

falling upon some method of recovering her
. . . will accommodate Mrs. Washington and lay
her under great obligation to you. . . .A
gentle reward will be given to any soldier
or other who shall take her up.' *

A spray of brown fluid splashed upon the publishing.
She tore it down from its post and ground it into
the dirt:

'I boot-blacked my face and hands
and any other parts that shows.
Ain't answerin to Charlotte, nigger,
nor no nother name they give me.
I'm wearing a westcoat and pants,
left the petticoat in a cornfield.
I'm 16. 13 was a lie the owner told
the auctioneer.
I'm evil, mean, and will use my knife.
I dips snuff, chews tobacco, smokes a pipe.
Ain't no son of satan gon fall on me lessn
he want his tail curled.
won't be intending toward no white folk
—all of ems enemies.
I'm headed West
I'll swim any river—maybe the Ohio—
follow any star.
And whoever try to take me up may
be ketchin his guts as he run.'

* Frank R. Stockton, "The Slaves of New Jersey," in *Stories of New Jersey* (Rutgers University Press, New Brunswick, N.J., 1961), p. 87. This book was originally published in 1896. This passage was reproduced by Stockton from a letter (c. 1777) written by one of George Washington's aides to a friend in Elizabethtown (Elizabeth, N.J.) on Washington's behalf when he was stationed in Morristown, N.J. The rest is the poet's fiction.

the layoff

A blizzard struck New Jersey like a tornado.
Snow accumulated like Chicago.
I saw a streak of lightning.
Someone else heard thunder.
I am earth and burned everything
I cooked tonight.
Managed to salvage a good slave's supper:
hoecake, turnip greens, navy beans.
In a month I get laid off.

Marijuana isn't what it used to be.
So I learn from poetry to reach for
the brief epiphany.

My parents each made their own money.
Raised me to make mine.
Worked at one job
in one office
in one building
slept in one bed for 35 years
so I could have choices.

Marijuana isn't what it used to be.

My sister the goddess of speech
got laid off last month.
She has a child.
And I want what's good for my poetry.

By turns I feel proud
politically correct
of the masses
then humiliated
humbled
and by turns

find myself in a daze
rapt
on how I'll put gas in my car past June.
I want to hear no anecdotes about those
who have less.

Marijuana isn't what it used to be in this
era of the nuclear renaissance white boy.

DINA COE

Manhattan, Now That I Don't Live There

I'm going to dive from the bus
halted in the roadcut
in tunnel traffic,
I'm going to dive into the frozen river
below the Holiday Inn, the big sign
advertising day rates,
and swim under to the city
erupted in crystals, an outcrop over there.
Sheer ones reflect the ice-blue dusk,
others have vanished in lights.
But how clearly
by the sky's pale vastness,
grime-black crevices define
the middle, red-brown mesas,
the upper and lower
igneous and metamorphic masses,
every needle and tooth.
I'm not as tender as I was,
and the majestic jutting of rock
fades to a tremor against the sky,
so little
between me and nothing. So,
because these stones of vanished cliffs remain
all that is there
beyond Newark and the oil refineries,
I'm going to swim under
the river of traffic, the filthy ice,
because they stand up—
high rocks where people must live
by their prayers.

Garden Journal, November

Two days out of three, it rains. I dig
a bed for Saint Patrick's Day planting.
The light is weak when I begin and fails
so fast, I feel off-the-subject considering
parsley, parsnips, potatoes, peas. The grey-
striped neighbor cats keep curling
out of a perpetual dusk to shit
milky diarrhea in the trench I've bared
by shovelfuls of mud. So long before the time
to set out lettuce, I look as if I'm digging
my own grave. I unearth roots and rocks,
hurl some at cats unfazed as spirits,
bend to line my ditch with leaves and bonemeal,
compost, lime, manure, ash. The mud
plants second soles on my shoes. Myself
a shadow in the twilight, dreaming of onions,
radishes and mustard greens, I lug my cart
to stables at the end of town, wade the liquid
gulley where the path drowned, pull away
summer's creaking pokeweed from the dung hill,
and fill and pull my cart back. I wrench my
back and spend the day in a rocking chair,
icepacked, in the dank house. (Can't bear
starting the furnace with winter yet to come.)
My back still bad, I have to sneak
past D.K. to work, digging from a crouch.
D.K. is laying the floor
in the new room of our house. He's upstairs and cosy
where the lamp is on. (I refuse to light
lamps this early in the day.) His work is hard:
forcing boards to lock, countersinking
nails. Beneath his feet, a solid floor
expands. My bed grows by unnoticeable inches.
I often feel I'm drifting like the fallen leaves,
wanting to think of something else than spinach.
My gloves are hands of coldest mud. I could go

into the kitchen, submit to light, cook something
that takes pleasant hours to the radio's barrage
of news no darkness ever slows. But I see
corn salad, that touseled mop: some green
exquisite animal from the melting snow. Better
to stay squatting, while I'm woman enough
and able, by November's smokey river, and dip
my shovel and turn and pull it with the current.

Midsummer's Eve Day

The path is almost hidden in grass on this
longest day like one green-blue night; daisies
come out like stars to the rim of the field.
As always at this time, the indigo bunting
hurls from cover to cover, through the gold
in the light. A handfull or spitball of gleaming
cobalt I'd say, remembering the goblins
padding the silver mines of the stories
under the waist-high flowers. I wade down
the deep bowl, two blackbirds fly low,
the green berries will soon be black fruit.
The stream flows slowly, auburn and oily,
sprouted with reeds, turning its water blades.
The colors are so strong, the stream bottom
peaks like a summit under my legs. I bend down
to the dragonflies which tremble and vanish
like popped bubbles when examined, like water dryads
in a picture in a book. I didn't have my baby,
having nowhere to go. Not having, having,
and now here where the earth is so full.
What a huge, hard, concave blue is the sky
for illusion . . . . But it is quite real: see the blue

panes of pond slick caught on rushes, rocks.
They aren't mere reflections, their opaque surfaces
don't wrinkle on the current. They are anywhere I look
on midsummer's eve, when shards of the hollow
turn out of every bowl and cup.

TOI DERRICOTTE

To a Traveler

You are welcome at every house:

Once the door opens
It opens to receive
even our ugliness.

The feet of the traveler
Are black like a black man—
The traveler has been awaited
So long each
Word is poetry.

The smell of night
Like incense
Rumbles in our empty chest,
Though night has many hours
It is not too long.

Like the camel,
With our eyes open, we
Sleep in the cool
Summer rain:

        Night
opens its sweet legs,

We climb in.

advice to somebody waking up

first you learn to turn your
ears off in the morning, like lights,
listen to the bass drum rolling
like thunder in the white
room of your skull.
you take 6 cups of flour
& 1 cup of water & you make
bread, bread, bread.
you eat it up like dust in your throat
gagging on your nightmares
which are bones to be blessed
out of your throat.

The Friendship

I tell you I am angry.
You say you are afraid.
You take your glasses off and lay
them on the table like a sparkling weapon.
I hold my purse in front of me.
Do I love you? Do you love me?
"If we just had time . . ."

You could show me how you wore your hair
pushed forward over one eye,
hiding half of what you knew of beauty.

Poor friendship, why must it sit
at a table where the waitress
is ready to go home? In a city
between tunnels—
cracks of darkness in the sea.

Allen Ginsberg

Once Allen Ginsberg stopped to pee at a bookstore in
    New Jersey,
but he looked like a bum—
not like the miracle-laden Christ with electric atom juice, not
    like the one whose brain is a river in which was plunked
    the stone of the world (the one bathing fluid to wash away
    25,000 year half-lives), he was dressed as a bum.
He had wobbled on a pee-heavy bladder
in search of a gas station,
a dime store with a quarter booth,
a chinese restaurant,
when he came to that grocery store of dreams:
Chunks of Baudelaire's skin
glittered in plastic;
his eyes in sets, innocent
as the unhoused eyes of a butchered cow.
In a dark corner, Rimbaud's
genitals hung like jerky,
and the milk of Whitman's breasts
drifted in a carton, dry as talcum.
He wanted to pee and lay his head
on the cool stacks;
but the clerk took one look
and thought of the buttocks of clean businessmen squatting
    during lunch hour,
the thin flanks of pretty girls buying poetry for school.

Behind her, faintly,
the deodorized bathroom.
She was the one at the gate
protecting civilization.
He turned, walked to the gutter,
unzipped his pants and peed.
Do you know who that was?
A man in the back came forth.
Soon she was known as
the woman in the store on Main
who said no to Allen Ginsberg;
and she is proud—
so proud she told this story
pointing to the spot outside, as if
still flowed that holy stream.

The Struggle

We didn't want to be white—or did we?
What did we want?
How could I decipher
in the milk of regular four hour feedings?
In two bedrooms, side by side,
four adults, two children.
My aunt and uncle left before light.
My father went to the factory, then the cleaners.
My mother vacuumed, ironed, cooked,
pasted war coupons. In the afternoon,
she typed stencils at the metal kitchen table;
I crawled under pulling on her skirt.
What did we want?
As the furniture became modern, the carpet deep, the white
ballerina on the mantel lifted her arms like some girl near
terror;

the Degas ballerinas rested in a group, a gray sensual
beauty.
What clocks set us to rise, our parents not speaking,
and we cousins who mourned a child born before us, her
sister—a suggestion we were not guaranteed.
What did we push ourselves out of ourselves to do? Our
hands on the doors, cooking utensils, keys.
Our hands folding the paper money, tearing the bills.

Blackbottom: 1945

When relatives came from out of town,
we would drive down to Blackbottom,
drive slowly through the congested main streets—Beubian and
    Hastings—
trapped in the mesh of Saturday night.
Freshly escaped, black middle class,
we snickered, and were proud.
The louder the streets, the prouder.
We laughed at the bright clothes of a prostitute,
a man sitting mindless on the curb with a bottle in his hand.
We smelled barbecue cooking in dented washtubs and our
    mouths watered.
As much as we wanted it we couldn't take the chance.

Rhythm and blues came from the windows, the throaty voice of
    a woman lost in the bass, in the drums, in the dirty down and
    out, the grind.
"I love to see a funeral, then I know it ain't mine."
We rolled our windows down so that the waves rolled over us
    like blood.
We hoped to pass invisibly—
be members of that ritual release—knowing on Monday we
    would return safely to our jobs, the post office and classroom.

We wanted our sufferings to be offered up as tender meat,
and our triumphs to be belted out in raucous song.
We had lost our voice in the suburbs, in Conant Gardens,
    where each brick house delineated a fence of silence and a
    lawn on which it was impossible to walk;
we had lost the right to sing in the street and damn creation.

We returned to wash our hands of them,
to smell them
whose very existence
tore us down to the human.

Poem for My Father

You closed the door.
I was on the other side,
screaming.

It was black in your mind.
Blacker than burned-out fire.
Blacker than poison.

Outside everything looked the same.
You looked the same.
You walked in your body like a living man.
But you were not.

would you not speak to me for weeks
would you hang your coat in the closet without saying hello
would you find a shoe out of place and beat me
would you come home late
would i lose the key
would you find my glasses in the garbage
would you put me on your knee

would you read the bible to me in your smoking jacket after
     your mother died
would you come home drunk and snore
would you beat me on the legs
would you carry me up the stairs by my hair so that my feet
     never touch bottom
would you make everything worse
to make everything better

i believe in god, the father almighty,
the maker of heaven, the maker
of my heaven and my hell.

would you beat my mother
would you beat her till she cries like a rabbit
would you beat her in a corner of the kitchen
while i am in the bathroom trying to bury my head underwater
would you carry her to the bed
would you put cotton and alcohol on her swollen head
would you make love to her hair
would you caress her hair
would you rub her breasts with ben gay until she stinks
would you sleep in the other room in the bed next to me while
     she sleeps on the pull-out cot
would you come on the sheet while i am sleeping. later i look
     for the spot
would you go to embalming school with the last of my mother's
     money
would i see your picture in the book with all the other black
     boys you were the handsomest
would you make the dead look beautiful
would the men at the elks club
would the rich ladies at funerals
would the ugly drunk winos on the street
know ben
pretty ben
regular ben

would your father leave you when you were three with a mother
    who threw butcher knives at you
would he leave you with her screaming red hair
would he leave you to be smothered by a pillow she put over
    your head
would he send for you during the summer like a rich uncle
would you come in pretty corduroys until you were nine and
    never heard from him again

would you hate him
would you hate him every time you dragged hundred pound
    cartons of soap down the stairs into white ladies' basements
would you hate him for fucking the woman who gave
    birth to you
hate him flying by her house in the red truck so that the other
    father threw down his hat in the street and stomped on it
    angry like we never saw him
(bye bye
to the will of grandpa
bye bye to the family fortune
bye bye when he stomped that hat
to the gold watch,
embalmer's palace,
grandbaby's college)
mother crying silently making floating island
sending it up to the old man's ulcer

would grandmother's diamonds
close their heartsparks
in the corner of the closet
yellow as the eyes of cockroaches?

Old man whose sperm swims in my veins,

come back in love, come back in pain.

STEPHEN DUNN

Toward the Verrazano

Up from South Jersey and the low persistent
pines, pollution curls into the sky
like dark cast-off ribbons
and the part of us that's pure camera,
that loves funnel clouds and blood
on a white dress, is satisfied.
At mile 127, no trace of a tree now,
nothing but concrete and high tension
wires, we hook toward the Outerbridge
past Arthur Kill Road where garbage trucks
work the largest landfill in the world.
The windscreens are littered, gorgeous
with rotogravure sections, torn love
letters, mauve once-used tissues. The gulls
dip down like addicts, rise like angels.
Soon we're in traffic, row houses, a college
we've never heard of stark as an asylum.
In the distance there it is, the crown
of this back way in, immense, silvery,
and in no time we're suspended
out over the Narrows by a logic linked
to faith, so accustomed to the miraculous
we hardly speak, and when we do
it's with those words found on picture postcards
from polite friends with nothing to say.

Response to a Letter from France

*"We're living in a Socialist paradise.
My mind boggles when I think where
you live."*

All the trees are in bloom
though the gypsy moths, with their plague
mentality, are blossoming too.
Don't feel sorry for us. We've even learned
to live amid Republicans; the avarice
of gypsy moths is only a little more
mindless, effective. It's okay here.
The ocean isn't perfectly clean
but on good days when I get low enough
the waves push me out ahead of them;
lacking wings or an engine
it's the closest thing to flight.
In France, where life and theory
touch now and then,
I don't doubt your pleasures. But here
there's room enough for incorrect
behavior, which some of us plan on.
There are casinos and fifty or sixty miles
of pines to get lost in.
Socialism makes good sense, sure.
But we actually have four people
who love us, the tennis courts aren't
crowded, our neighbor who has no politics
was generous yesterday for other reasons.
At another time I would offer you
what falls short of promise, the America
outside of me and my part in it.

But not when you feel sorry for us.
I just killed a Brown Recluse spider.
The sun is out. I want you to know
the afternoon is ablaze with ordinary people,
smiling, full of hidden unfulfillment,
everywhere, my friend, everywhere.

South Jersey
July 15, 1981

Beyond Hammonton

Night is longing, longing, longing,
beyond all endurance.
—Henry Miller

The back roads I've traveled late
at night, alone, a little drunk,
wishing I were someone
on whom nothing is lost,

are the roads by day I take
to the car wash in Hammonton
or to Blue Anchor's
lawnmower repair shop
when the self-propel mechanism goes.

Fascinating how the lamplight
that's beckoned
from solitary windows
gives way to white shutters

and occasionally a woman
in her yard, bending over
something conspicuously in bloom.

So much then is duty, duty, duty,
and so much
with the sunvisor tilted
and destination known
can be endured.

But at night . . . no, even at night
so much can be endured.

I've known only one man
who left the road,
followed an intriguing light
to its source.
He told me
that he knocked many times
before it became clear to him
he must break down the door.

Between Angels

Between angels, on this earth
absurdly between angels, I
try to navigate

in the bluesy middle ground
of desire and withdrawal,
in the industrial air,
among the bittersweet

efforts of people to connect,
make sense, endure.
The angels out there,
what are they?

Old helpers, half-believed,
or dazzling better selves,
imagined,

that I turn away from
as if I preferred
all the ordinary, dispiriting
tasks at hand?

I shop in the cold
neon aisles
thinking of pleasure,
I kiss my paycheck

a mournful kiss goodbye
thinking of pleasure,
in the evening replenish

my drink, make a choice
to read or love or watch,
and increasingly I watch.
I do not mind living

like this. I cannot bear
living like this.
Oh, everything's true
at different times

in the capacious day,
just as I don't forget
and always forget

half the people in the world
are dispossessed.
Here chestnut oaks
and tenements

make their unequal claims.
Someone thinks of betrayal.
A child spills her milk;
I'm on my knees cleaning it up—

sponge, squeeze, I change nothing,
just move it around.
The inconsequential floor
is beginning to shine.

Atlantic City

To stare at the ocean in winter
    is to know
        the variety in repetition.

It's to understand repetition's secret
    link with solace.
        How often I went to it, lonely,

wanting its sexual music, its applause.
How often it took my mood
and deepened it, instructed me

loneliness is nothing special,
that I was anybody, a man.
Yesterday at the blackjack table,

a few hundred yards from the shore,
I doubled-down with eleven
and drew a three. That was it.

I walked up North Carolina to Arctic
all alone. The wind suggested
wonderful movement at sea.

I didn't care. I didn't care if
the waves were high and white
or if the seagulls

were dropping clam shells from the sky.
I had a loser's thought: how wise I was
for not paying to park.

That's what I said to myself
far away from myself
with the ocean now two blocks away;

how wise I was. The houses started to speak
of ruin. Boards on some windows.
Wine bottles in doorways.

To stare at a city half in ruin,
half in glitter,
is to know why the beach

and its beautiful desolation in winter
   is a fearsome place
     if one risks being calm and clear.

I wish I could say I turned around.

SEAN T. FARRAGHER

Snowman

for Caroline

One winter
my wife and I
built a snowman
of ice and string

the melting snow
bled into the Hudson
the roots of thin
steel beasts watched us
from their berth

the haze in a yellow arc
shivered with glass eyes—
the red wail of sirens
bit into our clasped hands

that night in our bed
her fingers with their
many silvered rings
sought my hair
then my tongue
grew into her bristle,
into slipping teeth

Our baby's hand reached through the womb,
and that winter ended.

2.

Five years
after
I write this
letter to her
old voice in my skin

I tie her plaid scarf
to my wrist,
I watch smoke
spring between red/blue gables

that Hudson,
that old oak shakes
the hung dead from arms and canyons
of snow belting ice in my hair

I remember black stones
in the Snowman's face;
a scarf and a crooked hat
we set between the twigs

We hugged snow in our shirts,
wrestled with our wet skin until
the ice kiss rubbed us
to a silent stare,
as blood blew my tongue
to her blood;
our hair shone in crisp pentangles,
cut jewels glistened in skin

I remember those
dry hands that leapt out
from my hair.
I crawl to the Hudson,
to stare at ice sheets,
and I play with the photo
of her face, that haunts my wall

3.

In my window
a woodsman
bangs his shovel
hard into ice
to cut steps home,
to pack the snow
into ruts for boots
and sleighs,
to grey and melt
with cinders and mud,—
then to drift
eventually
to that Hudson

At my desk
I search inside the wooden box
where I keep silk and string;
pearl buttons from the Snowman's coat.

I remember
the holes her red boots cut
in clean snow.

I speak for a snowbeast
I can no longer
rub into magic

One winter
my wife and I
built a snowman
of ice and string

from patches of talk
and often lies.

Modern Rivers

for Zoe

> *This Hudson*
> *This awful fish;*
> *sleek in its tongue,*
> *tender in its mouth,*
> *wet from dear fingers*

First, Woman:

I began above you
in the passage
of waves upon waves
I hear your eyes turn,
race to the chatter of muscles;

Inside,
body upon body;
my face rests
at the night
of your smile;
your legs quit;
your heat slows,
an hallucination
for the hereafter

I am long past hunger

2.

In your kiss,
I speak pressed
to the below of your legs,—
your arms a lost space
before separation

I am a forgotten space
before divorce

In the historical self
I am not last there

(or above you)

Here with the before woman
and the afterwards—

I love the odor of loss,
a late walk when the air is plenty,
and the miracle has two faces

I am quiet in my mask—
beauty entangled
in the sin of tenderness

such dishonor
when the water
crowds upon us

passion of change
is forever a blossom
of a woman dressed
in wonderful.

Then Man:

I was truth.
I wanted miracles
all forms of love
and abundance—
rest here,
take home the delight
of husband and father

I am them.

2.

I knew how I loved some
of all faces, longer and smaller
the turn of all voices;
above the journey I am older,
forgotten when angry—
I know she loves me.
It is irreverent to ask
again about patience

Once, she slept in my arms;
We rested through darkness,
beyond windows to enchantment;
no proof for amusement—
only the wait
of great divers
for the crease
in the cliff
to be swallowed

then regression,
a pause before exile.

3.

My dear friends
we are the safety of passion
above modern rivers

fate is alone when we meet

Then the River

> In cold Hudson,
> no witness
> but November

Above the Mountains
that look like trees

dark appears to itself

all mist lost
the river, gray,
its blood brown—
the waters move
through my hand
where I glide
down clean rocks
below the face
my love gave me

I learn how to fly
this last November

How easy to swim
above the horizon

2.

The river is awhile
in the trance of morning

The river within
is a slight
reorder of motion

Breached by the flood
a blank age
appears to itself

honor and glory
reserved for our turn
downstream,
where the tide
is chance,
and I am not found—
my body has no witness

fantasy is terror
the rivers never
stop watching

the mountain has feet
and fancy no shudder

I examine the manner
of my listening

The Hudson arranged
in pure spirit

great is the sigh.

ALLEN GINSBERG

Garden State

It used to be, farms,
stone houses on green lawns
a wooded hill to play Jungle Camp
asphalt roads thru Lincoln Park.

The communists picnicked
amid spring's yellow forsythia
magnolia trees & apple blossoms, pale buds
breezy May, blue June.

Then came the mafia, alcohol
highways, garbage dumped in marshes, real
estate, World War II, money
flowed thru Nutley, bulldozers.

Einstein invented atom bombs
in Princeton, television antennae
sprung over West Orange—lobotomies
performed in Greystone State Hospital.

Old graveyards behind churches
on grassy knolls, Erie Railroad
bridges' Checkerboard underpass
signs, paint fading, remain.

Reminds me of a time pond's pure
water was green, drink or swim.

Traprock quarries embedded
with amethyst, quiet on Sunday.

I was afraid to talk to anyone
in Paterson, lest my sensitivity
to sex, music, the universe, be discovered &
I be laughed at, hit by colored boys.

"Mr. Professor" said the Dutchman
on Haledon Ave. "Stinky Jew" said
my friend black Joe, kinky haired.
Oldsmobiles past by in front of my eyeglasses.

Greenhouses stood by the Passaic in the sun,
little cottages in Belmar by the sea.
I heard Hitler's voice on the radio.
I used to live on that hill up there.

They threw eggs at Norman Thomas the Socialist speaker
in Newark Military Park, the police
stood by & laughed. Used to murder
silk strikers on Mill St. in the twenties.

Now turn on your boob tube
They explain away the Harrisburg
hydrogen bubble, the Vietnam war,
They haven't reported the end of Jersey's gardens,

much less the end of the world.
Here in Boonton they made cannonballs
for Washington, had old iron mines,
spillways, coach houses—Trolleycars

ran thru Newark, gardeners dug front lawns.
Look for the News in your own backyard
over the whitewashed picket fence, fading signs
on upper stories of red brick factories.

The Data Terminal people stand on Route 40
now. Let's get our stuff together. Let's
go back Sundays & sing old springtime music
on Greystone State Mental Hospital lawn.

Spring 1979

We Rise on Sun Beams and Fall in the Night

Dawn's orb orange-raw shining over Palisades
bare crowded branches bush up from marshes—
New Jersey with my father riding automobile
highway to Newark Airport—Empire State's
spire, horned buildingtops, Manhattan
rising as in W. C. Williams' eyes between wire trestles—
trucks sixwheeled steady rolling overpass
beside New York—I am here
tiny under sun rising in vast white sky,
staring thru skeleton new buildings,
with pen in hand awake . . .

December 11, 1974

To Aunt Rose

Aunt Rose—now—might I see you
with your thin face and buck tooth smile and pain
            of rheumatism—and a long black heavy shoe

for your bony left leg
limping down the long hall in Newark on the running carpet
past the black grand piano
in the day room
where the parties were
and I sang Spanish loyalist songs
in a high squeaky voice
(hysterical) the committee listening
while you limped around the room
collected the money—
Aunt Honey, Uncle Sam, a stranger with a cloth arm
in his pocket
and huge young bald head
of Abraham Lincoln Brigade

—your long sad face
your tears of sexual frustration
(what smothered sobs and bony hips
under the pillows of Osborne Terrace)
—the time I stood on the toilet seat naked
and you powdered my thighs with calamine
against the poison ivy—my tender
and shamed first black curled hairs
what were you thinking in secret heart then
knowing me a man already—
and I an ignorant girl of family silence on the thin pedestal
of my legs in the bathroom—Museum of Newark.

Aunt Rose
Hitler is dead, Hitler is in Eternity; Hitler is with
Tamburlane and Emily Brontë

Though I see you walking still, a ghost on Osborne Terrace
down the long dark hall to the front door
limping a little with a pinched smile
in what must have been a silken
flower dress

welcoming my father, the Poet, on his visit to Newark
—see you arriving in the living room
dancing on your crippled leg
and clapping hands his book
had been accepted by Liveright

Hitler is dead and Liveright's gone out of business
The Attic of the Past and *Everlasting Minute* are out of print
Uncle Harry sold his last silk stocking
Claire quit interpretive dancing school
Buba sits a wrinkled monument in Old
Ladies Home blinking at new babies

last time I saw you was the hospital
pale skull protruding under ashen skin
blue veined unconscious girl
in an oxygen tent
the war in Spain has ended long ago
Aunt Rose

Paris, June 1958

from *Reading Bai Juyi*

VIII. TRANSFORMATION OF BAI'S
"A NIGHT IN XINGYANG"

I grew up in Paterson New Jersey and was
just a virginal kid when I left
forty years ago. Now I'm around the world,
but I did go back recently to visit my stepmother.
Then I was 16 years old, now I'm fifty eight—
All the fears I had in those days—I can still see myself
daydreaming reading N.Y. Times on the Chinese rug on the
living room

floor on Graham Avenue. My childhood houses are torn down,
none of my old family lives here any more,
mother under the ground in Long Island, father underground
near the border of Newark where he was born.
A highway cuts thru the Fair Street lot where I remember our earliest
    apartment, & a little girl's first kiss. New buildings rise
    on that street,
all the old stores along Broadway have disappeared.
Only the Great Falls and the Passaic River flow
noisy with mist then quietly along the brick factory sides
as they did before.

                                                    10:15 p.m.

After Rewi Alley's *Bai Juyi, 200 Selected Poems* (Beijing: New World
Press, 1983), p. 303.

from *Don't Grow Old*

I

Old Poet, Poetry's final subject glimmers months ahead
Tender mornings, Paterson roofs snowcovered
Vast
Sky over City Hall tower, Eastside Park's grass terraces & tennis
    courts beside Passaic River
Parts of ourselves gone, sister Rose's apartments, brown
    corridor'd high schools—
Too tired to go out for a walk, too tired to end the War
Too tired to save body
too tired to be heroic
The real close at hand as the stomach
liver pancreas rib
Coughing up gastric saliva
Marriages vanished in a cough
Hard to get up from the easy chair

Hands white   feet speckled   a blue toe   stomach big   breasts
 hanging   thin
hair white on the chest
too tired to take off shoes and black sox

II
He'll see no more Times Square
honkytonk movie marquees, bus stations at midnight
Nor the orange sun ball
rising thru treetops east toward New York's skyline
His velvet armchair facing the window will be empty
He won't see the moon over house roofs
or sky over Paterson's streets.

New York, February 26, 1976

III
Wasted arms, feeble knees
  80 years old, hair thin and white
    cheek bonier than I'd remembered—
head bowed on his neck, eyes opened
  now and then, he listened—
 I read my father Wordsworth's *Intimations of Immortality*
". . . *trailing clouds of glory do we come*
  from God, who is our home . . ."
    "That's beautiful," he said, "But it's not true."

"When I was a boy, we had a house
  on Boyd Street, Newark—the backyard
    was a big empty lot full of bushes and tall grass,
 I always wondered what was behind those trees.
When I grew older, I walked around the block,
  and found out what was back there—
    it was a glue factory."

May 18, 1976

. . . .

VI

Near the Scrap Yard my Father'll be Buried
Near Newark Airport my father'll be
Under a Winston Cigarette sign buried
On Exit 14 Turnpike NJ South
Through the tollgate Service Road 1 my father buried
Past Merchants Refrigerating concrete on the cattailed marshes
past the Budweiser Anheuser-Busch brick brewery
in B'Nai Israel Cemetery behind a green painted iron fence
where there used to be a paint factory and farms
where Pennick makes chemicals now
under the Penn Central power Station
transformers & wires, at the borderline
between Elizabeth and Newark, next to Aunt Rose
Gaidemack, near Uncle Harry Meltzer
one grave over from Abe's wife Anna my father'll be buried.

July 9, 1976

VII

What's to be done about Death?
Nothing, nothing
Stop going to school No. 6 Paterson, N.J., in 1937?
Freeze time tonight, with a headache, at quarter to 2 A.M.?
Not go to Father's funeral tomorrow morn?
Not go back to Naropa   teach Buddhist poetics all summer?
Not be buried in the cemetery near Newark Airport some day?

Paterson, July 11, 1976

I Love Old Whitman So

Youthful, caressing, boisterous, tender
Middle aged thoughtful, ten thousand noticings of shore ship
    or street,
workbench, forest, household or office, opera—

Allen Ginsberg 69

that conning his paper book again to read aloud to those few
    Chinese boys & girls
who know enough American tongue to ear his hand—
loath to select one leaf from another, loath to reject a
    sympathetic page
—the tavern boy's look, a stone prisoner's mustache-sweat,
    prostitute in the sun, garrulous old man waving goodbye on
    the stoop—
I skim *Leaves* beginning to end, this year in the Middle
    Kingdom
marvel his swimmers huffing naked on the wave
and touched by his desperado farewell, "Who touches this book
    touches a man"
tip the hat on my skull
to the old soldier, old sailor, old writer, old homosexual, old
    Christ poet journeyman,
inspired in middle age to chaunt Eternity in Manhattan,
and see the speckled snake & swelling orb earth vanish
after green seasons Civil War and years of snow
white hair.

Baoding, China, November 20, 1984

Written in My Dream by W. C. Williams

"As Is
you're bearing

a common
Truth

Commonly known
as desire

No need
to dress

it up
as beauty

No need
to distort

what's not
standard

to be
understandable.

Pick your
nose

eyes ears
tongue

sex and
brain.

to show
the populace

Take your
chances

on
your accuracy

Listen to
yourself

talk to
yourself

and others
will also

gladly
relieved

of the burden—
their own

thought
and grief.

What began
as desire

will end
wiser."

Baoding, November 23, 1984

After Whitman & Reznikoff

1

What Relief

If my pen hand were snapped by a Broadway truck
—What relief from writing letters to the *Nation*
disputing tyrants, war gossip, FBI—
My poems'll gather dust in Kansas libraries,
adolescent farmboys opening book covers with ruddy hands.

Lower East Side

That round faced woman, she owns the street with her three
    big dogs,
screeches at me, waddling with her shopping bag across
    Avenue B
Grabbing my crotch, "Why don't you talk to me?"
baring her teeth in a smile, voice loud like a taxi horn,
"Big Jerk . . . you think you're famous?"—reminds me of
    my mother.

April 29, 1980

MAX GREENBERG

Poem

        My function is to spot
irrelevance, to sound out the line,
see if the tone is off & how deep
digressions go.
        I can't say what this
takes out of me. It has deepened my
sense of time, especially those units
in which nothing happens.
        Discipline is the ethic
I have taken the time to sound out,
my own asthmatic pains
        that destroy time & fog
memory. My time & motion study
do not endear me to anybody.
I remain your luckless editor.
It was I, who suggested
breaking the tablets, the initial
thrust was erroneous, the tone harsh.
I suggested waiting a slave people out
but was caught up in
their madness, let my poetics
go. The man on the right
is me making a pig of myself.
        finally, I too
fell in with the rest & was dubbed
erev rav, those foredoomed to kill time.

An Ordinary Day

Barring all considerations
              the everyday man in me,
the unceremonious one,
needs looking after.
Hiking up the stairs
              on an ordinary day
makes nonlistening to good music
enervating as if genius were found
in a lower case band.
As princely as such a day is,
nothing grabs me
              history stale by now
dare be read as microfilm
and Pascal's letters to the Jesuits,
those brilliant epistles
need no answer
and the heart wrung on better days
is become a museum piece.
So much is skindeep. I feel no compunction
saying: someone should fly a flag
on an ordinary day with aplomb
as if to remind someone
that in ordinary times we need
a startling emblem, a little human
songster to belt it out,
a ballertistic policeman
directing traffic—
              an ordinary day
when a president confesses
to his bad side, showing
how we get brothers
when the hardnosed break up
and the stiff-necked
peel their skins.

The poet who
insists on magic, cunning and exile
must, I suppose, have his
unparalleled revelations while bathing
or lathering and quite suddenly feel the pinch
                    to make sense in a big way
on an ordinary day
when nothing has been blessed.

Hard Work

Stupid and incomprehensible,
with obscure notations,
as if the landscape were bandaged
waiting up for a master landscaper.

We can turn all this
around,
speak as between crumbling walls
turn and
            separate sheaves
that have already turned
moss color and even with the stench
high in me, make a new place
near the tulips
        that incredible life
            that defends itself adequately.

        Here, on hands and knees,
with bitterness and joy moving
I shall show my plight
and bring it from its haunts
to human scale.

Winter can no longer be
        the excuse. Here,
I shall make the work count.

The Pedestrian Holding Sway

Simple and direct minds
so that all is achievable
for the grasping: all ambivalence
out of the way, the terrible nuances,
frays escalating layer of meaning,
a slip more telling of how
the mouth goes about mouthing
and finds itself diverted at
the mercy of a calling beyond itself.
            What is there to talk about?
The insistent question when all opens
but the ground, a pig farm
growing dandelions fulsomely,
and the old stench hits you
and gets into your vest.
        What's not to like?
Given proportion and the feel
of the animal, would you guess mule?
Piglet? Or would you
move it along with the prelogical—
grunt of thunder, consuming fire,
the simpleminded roughhousing explanation—
as if eternal summer had come upon us slyly
and answers lay at hand.
Would you care to buy a sack of grain?

ALFRED STARR HAMILTON

Tenement

What do you know of sundown?
What do you know of our New Jersey iron saints?
What an ugly bunny!
What an ugly blotch!
Westside New Yorkers are at their windowpanes
The N.J. iron bunny is a visitor
The sun is hoarse visiting their windowpanes

Another evening is quieter
The sun isn't so uproarious
Jersey City is abounding in these lights
What are the inhabitants?
What names of old
Chirlandalo, Fra Lippi, and Mantagna's grocery store,
The name of Leonardo Da Vinci appears at a letter box at
    a doorway,
The green Madonna is on the lawn in some little park
    nearer by,
What a pageant just before dark
Only the poor know of such things
Only the poor know of this nativity
The sun that is red floods the pavements and the sidewalks
The sun creeps along these tenement vines
The sun visits these windowpanes this evening
The sun that is red falls on the floor
This is the night of our dear saviour's birth

Hoboken, N.J.

I know of a seaport
I know of a flour boat from Buffalo
I know of a sugar boat from the south
I·know of how many bags of flour
I know of how many bags of sugar
I believe in the Easter white rabbit
I believe in baking a cake
I know of how many longshoremen
I know of how many powdered bunnies

N.J. Belles Lettres

I know of a letter from the bunnies
I know of a letter from the coal mines
I know of a letter to the railroads
I know of a letter for F.O.B. fast delivery
I know of a letter full of love and kisses from Clementine
I know of one belle lettre to the N.J. iron bunny
I know of a letter to the toolmakers
I know of a letter to the other coal miners
I know of a letter to the coal heavers
I know of a letter to the firemen
I know of how many fiery furnaces
I know of how many smokestacks
I know of how many clouds up in the Jersey skies
I know of how many clouds of smoke all day long

Wind and Wheat

Nevertheless the wind is the friendly architect of the woods
Nevertheless the wind carves over daffodils that wave in
    the winds
The wind is at your front doorstoop—and you are to enter
The wind is curving of its architectural desires
The wind curves through your parlor ways tomorrow and
next day
The wind leaves off again, diminishes, and then
begins its work again
That the wind is of the past and the present and the future
Has carved your blood ancestors
Has carved our lives of what they have been
The wind is of the past and the present and the future
The wind is still more so of the future
Whichever way the winds will be curving presently
And leave us in our parlors
And the wind carves wheat
And curves our barn doors
The wind and the sun have played on our harvests
Today and tomorrow and Sunday
Will carve of our generations to be
Whichever way the winds will be curving presently,
When and all tomorrow's wind is diminishing, and then
Begins its work again
Over our lives, and carves our green gardens
And curves the loaves of the field that are to be sent to us

Night

I kept a typewriter
I carried a little dark suitcase around
I asked the proprietor for some or a little space
I was a stranger
I was always moving about
I knew there was lightning on the moon
I hammered golden letters against the wilderness
I hammered golden letters against the night
I held this light to myself
I had so little to say to all the rest

JIM HANDLIN

Weathervane Poem

End a sentence with a weathervane.
Hear its swallow tails creaking
On top of a red clapboard house
whenever the wind blows.
Let it be a metaphor for the mind
on mornings that are instinctual:
the body moving from one habit to another.
Coffee percolating on a big black stove.
The kittens pushing each other
around a saucer of milk, wanting more.
Who has the energy to let the bee out
that comes in with the dog
or wipe up his muddy footprints.
It's enough to pile strawberries
onto cornflakes, stick your arm
into the shadow patterns on the windowledge
and watch the wind blow the backs
of the leaves silver.

Akbar's Algebra

The shape of the Arabic letters
in his manuscript is
a perfect abstract of the waterfront
between Hoboken and Newark.

I have only to look up
and find a cupola collapsed
in front of a smoke stack,
a sky the color of glue.

Akbar brings Turkish coffee.
He's up from the South,
a convert to Islam. We talk.
In a perfect language, he says,
there'd be a way to square
the meaning of a word. There'd
be inflections for nostalgia.

Apple recalls October days
rotting away, bees swarming
in a yard too dangerous
to walk in. But Pear is
the street in Memphis
where Ruby lived, a pattern
of wallpaper and her breasts
yellowed by the morning light.

A History of Landscape

Distance makes the cows look stiff.
Closer a cook dressed in white
returns from the barn with a basket of eggs.
They look warm speckled with straw.

By turning the mirror
I could tilt the landscape, put the windmill
on its side so it becomes
a propeller.

But I choose the noise
that makes six crows
fly from the field into the woods.
The crows are its echo.

Still Life with a Fish Skeleton

On the platter under the skeleton
of the bluefish we've eaten
are pagodas
and a peasant with a coolie hat
poling a boat.
It is thirteenth century China,
imitation Sung Dynasty.
Shadows from fish bones suggest
pine trees, an early morning sun,
that nature is commenting on itself;
on the way we caught the bluefish
earlier this morning,
the great skeleton of stars
disappearing above us
as we rowed out
into the current.

Three Hours after Dawn

On the porch grandfather cleans his pipe.
The parts lie on a handkerchief.
He pushes the wire into them: it comes out
like a root pulled from black earth.

The tea kettle whistles from the kitchen.
The dog knocks over a vase
of blackeyed susans. Everybody shouts.
Since yesterday my voice is caught in my stomach.
Andy brings a pail of blackberries
from the woods behind the house.
There'll be fresh cream, butter, hot biscuits
for breakfast. They talk about the size
of the mushrooms, the nap of the moose's fur,
the way the lichen clings to the trees:
grandfather predicts the winter's snowfall.
But I keep remembering the rifle shots,
watch in slow motion the moose slump to his knees,
spring up, fall dead on the run
just before he reaches the river.

Remnants

1

Everything gets slow, stops.
I reread the telegram.

2

I remember the squirrel dead
at the end of the driveway.
The body thrown up on the grass
next to the azalea.
The red where the car hit
so different from the red
of the bush.
All that day and the next
I thought of ways
to stay close to my mother.

3

They auction the contents
of the estate. Limoges and
cloisonné, piece after piece.
The bed she slept in, her silver
tea set. I notice cobwebs
in corners, dust, places
where the wallpaper's faded.
Her painting for some other wall,
her gold for someone else's finger.
Outside tail lights slash the night:
red and more red.

No Names

We don't have names
for what goes on inside,
for the transformations
from fish to lizard to human.

I remember listening to my sister's
heartbeat, feeling the kicking.
Trying to understand
I watched the maple tree turn red;
first a few leaves
then more red along the edges.
Overnight the green was gone.

Now the baby inside my wife
kicks me awake. I think
of picnics and comic books.
It's just too hard to think of somebody
swimming and changing faces
in the dark.

PENNY HARTER

A Man beside the New Jersey Turnpike, Easter Eve

Among the marshy meadow-lands and garbage hills,
this sudden patch of field grass
holds a listing row of hen-houses
old and gray, and a man
sprawled on a wooden seat of sorts,
its back a scaffolding shoulder high.

Arms flung up and over the crosspieces,
head lolling to one side,
he is so still,
framed between the sheds and a pick-up truck,
he must be a scarecrow.

But he is too fat for a scarecrow,
stomach yeasty in blue overalls.
And scarecrows hang on poles where something grows.

So he has to be a man,
asleep, or even dead
in a field beside the Turnpike,
the city's spires distant behind him;

he has to be a man,
legs spread in the weeds,
arms hanging over wooden bars,
and head fallen to one side,
facing the traffic.

At the Mall

At the mall the faces of young girls
look out beneath spiked hair,
cheeks streaked rosy and lips glazed with color
more arrogant than blood.
They giggle, eyes darting at the racks of cheap jeans,
and sweaters with loose necklines.
Their hands stroke the shiny synthetics, the soft wools.

Outside, the stars are doing business with other animals.
The comet drags its tail through the dark,
and across the highway gravestones flare in headlights.

Inside, two boys fall to the floor fighting.
Their friends tear them apart.
The girls crowd into a phone cubicle
to punch random numbers with painted nails
and hang up before someone—anyone—answers.

They scream.

The boys are eating ice cream by the fountain;
its bottom glows with the currency of wishes.

Reading the Tea Leaves

After winter rain
dead leaves have steeped
in the gutter.

Easter eggs dipped in this tea
would darken
to barnyard brown.

On the neighbor's lawn an inflated swan
adrift on a stake like a weathervane
wheels slowly to face us.

I bend over the puddle,
stir with one finger
the cold silt at bottom,

watching the shredded leaves rise,
swirl and settle, as if I were
shaking them in a tiny globe.

Mattress Fire

When I was a child, my father
lit a cigarette in the night
and fell back asleep,
his arm dangling over the edge,
his curled fingers holding fire.

My parents dragged his mattress to the bathtub.
Later, they pinned an old blanket, tight
around its sagging middle
where some stuffing had dissolved to soggy lumps.

For years I watched my mother
change the sheets on that burnt mattress,
smoothing them over the old blanket,
the charred hole in the striped ticking.

My mother changed the sheets on that mattress
even when cancer from three packs a day
began to burn my father's jawbone,
dissolve his soft palate;

even after surgery, when he nestled
into his new life, his body
finding the familiar hollows.

The mattress finally collapsed into itself
twenty years after he stopped smoking.

Somewhere, my father's mattress still burns,
smouldering in the dumps off the Turnpike
like those underground fires
they can't put out for years.

WILLIAM J. HIGGINSON

The Passaic Falls, October

The falls floods:
Spray rises at center where water falls only a few feet from the
artificial cut-stone lip, invention of engineers for a now-
defunct electrical plant, to the real crest of the mid-section,
the great Falls belly, pounding up curtains of wind-torn spray
now coming in puffs as if in the gorge depths a Nordic pipe
were smoked by these cliffs.
The narrow gorge-end, years of debris-fill usually all trickles like
hidden woods springs sixty feet down, now has its own rich
tone, only a bit higher pitched than the eighty-foot drop at
the far gorge-mouth. Broken from below dashed from above
water rushes white down the narrow trough toward the center
of the depths.
Places I have stood are under a foot or two of smooth round
glaze deep green and silty brown water rolling neatly over the
edge only to turn white froth and spray in a few feet of
falling.
Going over rough rocks jutting into the gorge skirting the
dozens of small puddles left by the furious rains of midday
glinting in bits of cloud-freed sunlight hard to see how far
anything is through spray and myriad needles of sunset rays.
Fishing trawler crew of twenty-one pulled into the North
Pacific off Hokkaido swimming in and out of lifeboats one
whole day and night in typhoon sea three dead of exposure
the livelihood of twenty families pulled down by the force we
rarely notice on supermarket shelves the neat tins of bonito
tuna albacore all arranged we think according to our fancy.

Death everywhere Death smiles at the poor chips we are cast
into the flood unnoticed by the flying axe-blade. God no
sweet greybeard rocking and smiling before the furnace we all
must enter swept on the tide or over the Falls through smoke
or simply dissolution; there is only the furnace and we think
we can cajole some old grate-keeper with a paltry bribe a
clink in the collection plate a burnt offering of some flesh
other than our own; we think he smiles on us but it is only
the flames that mirror his watery beard his blank eyes staring
dumb out of the fire-center calling us the more irresistibly to
our individual ends chips feeding the blaze ships swirled
down in the vortex of spinning boards old tires tree trunks and
an occasional fifty-five gallon drum bobbing into the slowly
swirling eddy of garbage beneath the rusting turbines of the
silent electrical plant.

The gorge waits:
A fiercely grayed, lean grandfather invites his two small
  grandsons to come over the wall, stare with him down into
  the deep pounding that is the Falls bottom.
He does not see the vision of the smile in that furnace the quiet
  eyes beckoning—I warn of the wind the slippery rocks and he
  turns, coming back over the wall toward the boys toward me
  grey eyes luminous through the smoky spray.
The boys are fearless.
He would have them walk every edge dance for joy on the
  slippery rock over eighty feet of falling water.
He grins at the mouth only in his irritation; they walk away
  from me giggling through the mist the boys along the top of
  the uneven stone wall over the long wet grass bending down
  into the spray.

The wind gusts:
There is no small boy rolling gently with the planks over the
  deep quiet bottom of the North Pacific three men crackling in
  the dark flames.
I smile in the wind and my lips curl back.
The log steps of the path shift underfoot in the moist earth.

Nanna's Soap

There were four cakes of it there,
        one place or another
                in her bathroom,
two used, two still fresh
        in their cardboard boxes:
                        'Yardley Old English Lavender
Fragranced Soap.'
        It was the one thing you could always
                give her for Christmas
and know she would want it
        again the next year,
                and the next.
She would hold it to her nose
        even before she unwrapped it
                and smile her pleasure.
Perhaps later she'd sigh,
        washing and remembering
                the sachet in the drawers
of her mother's fine bureaus
        brought over from England
                to the Connecticut farmhouse.

We found four cakes
        cleaning out her apartment
                some weeks after she died.
Never a squeamish one,
        she'd have approved
                the way I washed the used ones
and wrapped them all up
        in a bag to take home.
                Tonight in the shower
the first of the four
        laves sweat from my limbs;
                its bubbles grow intimate
before washing away,
        leaving just a faint trace
                of its scent on my skin.

William J. Higginson   93

Paterson:
Spring Exotic

for the Lenni-Lenape

near all the blooming
pink and fuchsia
at the monument
in Eastside Park
there is one native
white dogwood tree

Spring in Paterson, I

At the old police headquarters
two plain-clothes men
bring in three young men
dressed well and casually
the one in the shortest hair
talking on nervously
"You know Mike DeVita,
Mayor of Paterson?
Well he was my grandfather's
nephew and my family
is very good friends with—"
"Come along, Mr. Smith."
"Anyone got a light?
I gotta smoke quick
one last cigarette. . ."
"Come along, Mr. Smith."
into the old police headquarters.

Spring in Paterson, II

On the DAILY NEWS corner
of City Hall's small block
two men wrestle on their backs
legs interlocked driving
one another back and forth
like a Siamese twin crab.
The hairier one leaps up
driving the other's back
to the still frosty pavement—
ha HAAH—as the fellow
on his back rolls to the side
flails out a long leg almost
meeting the other's shin
high in the leap of a Cossack dancer
and a long black car
slowly rolls up to the bystanders
one of whom thrusts through
the open window a newspaper.

MARK HILLRINGHOUSE

In Paterson

for Tom Greco

As I stand here
on the corner of Market & Main
under the giant shadow of the Broadway Bank
gazing into shop windows, I feel like
one of those sixteenth century Dutch characters
so out of place in a crowd of local merchants
in one of Breughel's great paintings.
I wonder if there's a connection to anything
as I stand here with a headful of questions
like who put me in this picture?
when I should probably be off fishing somewhere
or finding my own place among the clouds
in another river-town surrounded by hills & factories.
Questions spilling out of my head
like the twin rivers of my desire,
one happy, one sad to be alone.
And I know there's a meaning to all this
now that you're gone,
even the buildings look tired
and the streets a little sadder,
even as I blend into this background
of weirdos & strangers
who stick their necks out like gargoyles
and shout obscenities from street corners,
even as I watch a man dressed for winter in the middle of July
dance to his own music in the reflection of Jacob's
Department Store, even as I enter Woolworth's to buy

something I don't need, another piece of grief
that'll end up as garbage on the streets
as a poor substitute for anger & despair
while others go around erecting huge monuments to their
    failures.
And out of all this decay & poverty,
the one event to make me smile all day,
a Spanish father bending over to hug & kiss his son
in the squalor of Grand Street,
knowing that we all begin and end pretty much in the
    same way,
and the difference a little love makes in our lives,
when I think of you sitting in your chair by the window
and the sunlight you slept in,
or when you stood behind the bar and gave us some comfort
for our troubles,
when all we talked about
was the boredom around us,
and the jobs we hated,
and the places we call home.

Cianci Street

for Linda

I love walking past the ugly stores
and staring into the dirty windows.

I love sitting here in the morning sun
with a warm cup of milk in my hands.

I love the muddy river, the seagulls
circling in the sky above me,
the sounds of traffic, the old men
shouting and cursing in Italian.

And I love the warmth of your smile,
the whole day in front of me
like a long blue shadow.

Dear Walt

Was thinking of you
as I sat on a bench facing the ocean.
I'd like to see you
right now walking through Paterson,
through the city Hamilton invented,
birthplace of the sweatshop
and the steam locomotive,
the expression on your face
changing from a look of wonder & awe
as you head down Market Street
waving to strangers.
I'd drive you down
the New Jersey Turnpike
over to Camden
to show you the rest area
named in your honor.
Or I'd take you out to Long Island
to the great American nightmare
of a shopping mall bearing your name
to show you what America
really thinks of you.
I can imagine you running with horror
from the fluorescent bulbs
and the glass walls.

You would see how useless & reckless
we've become.
I can picture you on the street
examining a piece of plastic,
so far from wood,
so unlike anything in nature.
Does it belong to the earth?
It has nothing to return to.
It will not feed the grass.

Leaving Paterson

I love this city by the falls
and all its constant trouble.
No one bothers me or bothers
to look at it the way I do.
I am happy here
even though I cannot write
about the way I feel.
I never grow tired of these streets
or the faded-green houses,
or the immigrant faces
peering through torn curtains
in the afternoon.
I love the river and all its rusted bridges.
No one sings of the vacant lots
covered with blue chicory,
or the winos asleep in their army coats
outside the Evergreen Liquor Store,
or the big breasted Hispanic
who dances all night naked for strangers
in the Doctor's Cave Topless Disco.
It is summer and the city is buried in ozone
and goes on with its business.
I turn left at an abandoned factory

Mark Hillringhouse 99

and past the mills,
driving out alone up Garrett Mountain
along the road that takes me home.
The buildings behind me disappear
into a coast of rooftops,
in a landscape of trembling daylight.

ELIOT KATZ

As I Stand Before Your Grave, Camerado
—LINES WRITTEN AT WHITMAN'S TOMB, JULY 5TH, 1986

Cheers, Walt! I raise my bottle of juice to you.
Ignored or worse in your life's time,
now you've made it:
superstar, the original American poet
    recognized by all.
Yet, as I stand before your grave, camerado,
how I grieve for you,
for your vision of America becoming just a dot
    in the universe's rearview mirror
as real U.S. drives further away every day
    from your dream of libertad.
Even as I stood last night
among half million mothers, daughters, fathers, sons,
Battery Park, Manhattan, cheering explosions
    of fireworks tremendous,
drunken happy, loud proud voices toasting
    Statue of Liberty's 100th birthday,
how sad I grew thinking how hidden true liberty today,
thinking your lines in Democratic Vistas
that in this great new country feudalism would end
or America would be the greatest failure
    of all time.

Walt, stand up! Can you walk a bit?
Stroll your body's final resting place,
Camden, New Jersey, once Garden State,
    now world's cancer capital.

Look with your love-of-workers eyes at homes built
        with broken boards on made-to-break foundations!
Try to treat with experienced nurse's hands
        the casualties of the USA's longest running
        undeclared war, the war on its own!
Try to treat the long suffering sufferers of the disease
        caused by extreme poverty of open space!
Pick up a few McDonald's wrappers and Pepsi cans
        loitering on sidewalks and in apartment hallways!
Inhale car and factory exhaust in the air
        you loved odorless and free!
Taste the water that doesn't even
        look like water anymore!

Walt, in your wildest prophetic imagination
        did you imagine the hydrogen bomb?
The Neutron Bomb? Plutonium waste dumps?
The country you loved atom bombing Hiroshima?
Acquiring wealth by arming tyrants
        Southeast Asia to Latin America?
Over a century after Lincoln, furthering Black
  American poverty
        and supporting Black South African slave systems?
Did you foresee 1986 USA stealing more land
        promised forever to its Native Americans?
Are your feet too tired to walk further, Walt?
and watch America's homeless driven with invisible
        economic psychological sadistic whips
        out of barely sheltering shelters
        from Santa Barbara, California
            to New Brunswick, New Jersey?
You wrote that in a generation or two there'd be
        no more priests,
        everyone his or her own priest.
Yet, today, guilt-inflicting grabbers
        of the names Morality and Religion
        grow richer denying Christ's concept of compassion
            than ever before!

You wrote liberty was preparing for us,
that liberty would not be first to leave earth,
nor second, but last, after all life
        in every form had already departed.
Now the U.S.S.R., another nation whose leaders
        have so far failed its great poetic vision,
and the U.S. run a weapons race
        that if not stopped
will surely destroy all earth lifeforms
        and as well your cherished liberty.
Yet, Walt, as I stand before your grave,
I can somehow feel your breath shooting through
        my feet ankles knees thighs balls ribs heart chest
        neck chin mouth eyes ears skull!
Oh, to look at the leaves around your tomb!
To touch with my hands
        the encasement of your dreams and desires
        for a just, uplifting America!
Walt, for as long as my body shall live
so shall your spirit and struggle
        for libertad!
I swear it! here and now!
        on your grave!
                camerado!

                                    1986

After Ten Years, So Long New Brunswick

I ran up nine flights
        of new office building stairs
and knocked furiously
on the door of the Spirit of New Brunswick.
Without waiting, I barged in.

She was sitting on a cushion of air
　　　behind an invisible desk.

"New Brunswick," I said,
"You've been better than all right
　　　but sometimes you can be
　　　　　one crazy spiritfucker."
"I'm St. Louis," the spirit answered,
　　　"You want the third door on your left."

In the hallway, a janitor stopped me
asking why the spirit of a town
　　　has to be a woman.
"It doesn't," I replied, "But the one
　　　I'm looking for is."

At New Brunswick's door I waited for an
　　　invitation to enter.
When I saw her, I wanted only
　　　a huge wordless hug.
But without speaking, she let me know
　　　her spirit body off limits,
　　　　　especially to a guy leaving town in three days.

"New Brunswick," I said, "tell me,
　　　the plusses and minuses,
　　　how have I served thee?"
"Well, E. Katz," she answered,
"You tried, but you were too awkward,
　　　you staggered and tripped on sidewalks,
　　　you finally got your finger caught
　　　　　in the printing press,
　　　you slurred your words,
　　　you developed a very strange laugh,
　　　you left boring messages on your
　　　　　telephone answering machine
　　　and you drank way too much."

"What about the plusses?" I asked.
She started, "Well, E. Katz, you tried
	but you were too awkward,
	you staggered and tripped on sidewalks,
	you . . ."

"Enough!" I stopped her.
"What about the poems?
What about the nine to fives,
the leaflets and resumes I printed
the humane politics
and the smiles, even though often drunken,
	that were always heart felt.

"The poems . . . okay.
Better than I thought possible eight years ago.
Everything else too impermanent.
From the resumes you printed people got shitty jobs.
From the leaflets people saw shitty bands.
Nine to fives worth even less
	than your paltry pay.
And the politics and smiles; genuine
	but short-lived.
E. Katz, you've left no legacy here."

"Well, I guess I've no reason to stay.
	So long New Brunswick."
I closed the door behind me—
then rushed back in.
"Won't you even miss me?"
	I demanded to know.

"You're awkward, but not that many even try."
She hugged me, kissed me once with her tongue,
	then kicked my ass out of there.
"Keep in touch," I screamed,
	speeding the invisible elevator nine floors down.

How Many More Nights?

He's about 60 years old, tall and lean
with gray beard and thinning gray hair.
Every day I see him drinking coffee
        outside the train station.
And every night on my way to Court Tavern
I see him sleeping outside
        under the roofed Ferren Parking Deck.
Tonight it's about zero degrees Fahrenheit
and he's got a woman in his arms
and a baby carriage a few feet away.
Does he know her? I wonder.
Or are they just friends for mutual warmth?
Does she know what he looks like in the day light?
Is there really a baby?
Or is the carriage just
        a shopping cart to carry her things?
They're covering themselves with a green army blanket.
How many wars has he fought for America?
Has America fought any wars for him?
How many wars has America's government
        fought against him?
How many more nights will
        he have the will
        to fight this war?
How many Americans will line up
        on his side?

1987

DAVID KELLER

Stopping for Breakfast

I'd seen the neon sign, bakery, and I stopped
more for the picnic table under a tree out back,
September, and the sky a blue I'd nearly forgotten.
I bought coffee and two sweet rolls and went outside
as if I were passing through, undecided where to go.
Across the highway was a field of something growing,
and next door, a tractor by the garage said whose house
that was. How out of place that machine looks: enormous,
ribbed tires and a rod from the steering wheel
the length of the body and down to the front wheels.
Those were small and pigeon-toed and I've learned that means
a John Deere. He must have made that first tractor
right from the idea, with whatever parts and things
he'd held onto. This one was garden green and yellow
for the wheels, to show how proud he was, the paint
he'd thought to keep, and they're still made that color.

The house was not one of those large farmhouses.
The lawn looked tiny, and a blue swimming pool
with a beach umbrella set up over a table said,
this is Jamaica, or any place but New Jersey fields
and roads, like a suit some men save
for Sundays to suggest they know how things might be.
Maybe he just wanted some shade to eat dinner
on the hot evenings. The tree I sat under was the closest.
It takes forty years to get them back
after the builders leave.
My mother would have pointed out whatever passed for beauty
along the roads on vacation, the hot fields

and momentary farms beyond them. Or she'd keep silent
at how much like where we lived it seemed.
She and my father moved to Iowa and stayed,
not quite settled among the towns and farms.
She liked mountains, or just that she hated
so much flat sky around. Improvement tugged her,
as a place life could be exciting, better for us.
Sometimes, when I think she's right
I am ashamed, like a child
caught peeing in the bushes by a younger sister.

A man walked out of that house, across the blacktop drive
and in the side door of the bakery with an empty cup,
as if it weren't unusual, just morning in this place
like the one I left. My mother finally moved back
to where she said she'd come from and shut the door.
The man walked out of the bakery, crossing the drive
and the yard with his cup full of coffee,
taking his time. The rolls weren't half bad.
That seemed about right
to describe the state of things this morning,
the world like a play in rehearsal, leading to this road
next to a roadside bakery and the coffee there
on a warm morning before that day went off on its own.
And this was where we were, the man who could own a green
and yellow John Deere, working the fields
of soybeans and corn between the freeways, called farms.
Slowly he closed his back door behind him,
so as not to spill and not to catch the world
in the door going out, like a cat's tail.

I come from Iowa, I tell people who ask,
like a missing country. I dropped the napkin and my cup
in the garbage can chained to the one tree,
the way my mother taught us, traveling the land
that wasn't ours, as if the trash would change
some balance, and she was eager to get on
to a place better for her

and for kids who didn't care if they grew up.
I took a look before heading on to work,
and it wasn't a bad spot, not bad.

Longing

Up the streets a solitary man is taking apart a machine
on his steps, the pieces set to either side of him.
From how he works with a pair of pliers, then
a screwdriver, and back, he's not used to this
though the work is absorbing.
Everywhere it is silent as she and I
finish our meal abruptly, after a sudden argument,
after the anger leaving a cold film on the plates.
She goes upstairs and shuts her sewing room door.
Outside the last light has finally worked its way
down the garden and the neighbor's trees, a day finished.

It might be a vacuum cleaner he's working on.
They are an easy machine to fix if you know the right screws
to get at the parts caught, jammed with the years
of dust we pick up from room after room.
It is good work, the company of your hands
demanding nothing more than to be present.
You wipe each part until the machine becomes a friend.
Afterwards it will fit back together exactly
as the maple next door fits the leaves each year.

If I could remember how to do it,
I could cross the street and show him the simplest way.
And the next time we passed each other he'd
stop to talk a little instead of exchanging a nod.
I'd ask if he knew how to end the irritation I feel
like grit cutting each night, long after sleep.

Perhaps his wife will know. And my wife would come
    downstairs
later, quietly over to the window and lean against me.
It would be something as simple as two neighbors
banter back and forth if the weather is good,
and I'd feel better about the year, about love
as I leave for work these half-dark mornings.
It would end this fever whirling around me.

The man's gone, the window cool on my forehead.
It doesn't seem such a big thing to imagine,
him sitting out back now and the evening's coffee
warm between his hands. That's how I'd like it.
The light is good of a Sunday evening, the yard
like fields I remember, a place I was happy with her.
And I hear something that might bring a smile
to the neighborhood this time of the day, the sound
of someone singing to themselves, cleaning a house.

Going Back to the City

The sun
has finished the small buildings, and the light
recedes, heading toward the bridges.
It has been years. Coming back
today was not the memory
of what you'd left here or taken to the next place,
but as if the streets you, too, passed
were someone else's life entered,
by mistake you'd say, tired from walking.
A woman sweeps off the steps,
the familiar spirit of the neighborhood,
but doesn't look up. The clouds
are colored paper. What's puzzling

is how the buildings are part of the sunset
sinking down one wall then the next.
Suddenly everything is changed, one skyscraper
electric blue, silver, rising beyond shoppers
and the man selling magazines. It glows
like a river seen from distant hills.

In the town where you were young, fireflies
rose from the grass like sparks.
Some nights your parents
would forget about you altogether
and you and your three brothers would follow
the lights long after bedtime
as they moved off, higher
around the house and into the treetops.
You might have been leaving with them.
First the driveway, then the bushes
by the mailbox lost to sight,
the house and its lights fading
in the warm, dark air,
and that reflection in the building,
the city you no longer need close by.
Oh, that is it come
back to you now: the world
inside you rising, tall buildings,
this sharp blue light and beyond, the sky.

The Chinese Written Character as a
Medium for Poetry

I still think I remember some old mechanic
or a farmer using Coca Cola
to clean the rust off metal parts.

Teachers would hand out that stuff
as a warning to convince the kids
to take up a life of reading the classics.
Like the rest, I, too, have let things slide,
so that summer, for example, is no more
than an ad in the smoking car,
tanned couples playing outdoors.

At night even the metaphors are tired
of how their jobs have become petty
and badly paid, the respect lessened.
It is true. At times I ache to see things
so clearly as they seemed to those teachers,
to remember for future nights.
How I disliked their prudish
insistence on manners and dull clothes.

All this happened on the train to Newark,
where it still hurts to think how much
has been burned or built over, the poverty.
Nobody reads much, romances, the paper.
It was hot as hell. One ad showed a couple,
cigarettes and, from their smiles, plenty
of vegetables. But some kid had reached
down into his useless relic of a memory
and had written on the poster
It Dirt Weed, and it surely is.

Crossing the States

Easy as walking the railroad
one night with friends. There is such light
it shines out from dry cornstalks
to the sky. Anything might happen,

such evenings, and be welcome.
Out over the bridge, the foolish highway
then the full moon, the hunter's moon,
anchored in the oily river.
We cross into Pennsylvania in the air.
A rock thrown far out still misses,
but ripples lift and bother the light.
The dog dislikes the rough ties, the spaces
filled with sharp ballast,
and walks too close to the railing.
It's all right, say the others.

In the shadow and blue light of our bodies,
I imagine new selves without any harm
to them, or injury, but still like us.
They hold silence as people holding hands,
the rocks and islands blossoming on the river.
That is what bridges are for,
the long drive with my family on vacation,
like pioneers in the schoolbooks
to say we aren't really from Iowa
then repeat it, the hours
to get as far as the immense brown river and Omaha.
No one had told me it was so much wider
than a river, to someplace different
I hoped my parents might like.

If we turn back, it is
that tomorrow there's work and the railroad
goes barely as far as Philadelphia.
The dog's shadow moves out ahead,
she would gladly amble into past or future
along the tracks and keep on.
I am older than my father
in those days. I take one last look,
the trees rising on either side, the land
climbing back to the bridge's end to meet us.
Here are friends, it says.

You are where you are, the moon repeats,
and its reflection in the sky.
The air is sharp, we hurry,
even the shining fields gray, salt water.

At the Edge of the Continent

The shore, it's called here, where the women
with children dancing in and out of the waves
at the sand's sloping edge are tired and don't
know it, or pretend not to see their thighs
and the backs of knees thickened, losing their hold.

Even their faces show traces of some
previous incarnation still not quite at ease.
The children are too busy, joyous or whiny
in love with their mothers; they do not care.
Their fathers with red arms look on, aloof,

and whatever they think of, say nothing.
Of how the 17-year cicadas, alive all spring
must have been here when I was twelve, and again
at twenty-nine, though not where I grew up.
Would I have noticed? These insects seem not to,

or worry they might miss out on a new cure,
a film to explain everything that was
in doubt or seemed lost. Filling the streets
with enormous noise, they don't eat or mate.
Even their single-minded flights do not

take heed of strangers, or others like themselves.
After awhile I stopped being frightened.
Their red wooden eyes and bright black bodies,

even the wings with their ribs and bright, oak
leading edge seem props made for an old film

and the children we must have been in those years.
Some of the women complain, of the chances passed
to dance or paint, among the kitchen routines;
They desire something lost for their efforts,
some promise made to stay with them forever

the husbands and those children have not kept.
Our fathers kept silent, if they knew anything,
beyond noticing a son's shoulders, a daughter's smile,
these offspring more beautiful than their parents
and what that might say about the passing time.

In the stillness, whatever drove the cicadas
has gone again, the offspring they set out
unconcerned as the trees. What they hoped for
in this strange world and its sky full of objects
flying will take a while to tell us.

BRIGIT PEGEEN KELLY

Doing Laundry on Sunday

So this is the Sabbath, the stillness
in the garden, magnolia
bells drying damp petticoats

over the porch rail, while bicycle
wheels thrum and the full-breasted tulips
open their pink blouses

for the hands that pressed them first
as bulbs into the earth.
Bread, too, cools on the sill,

and finches scatter bees
by the Shell Station where a boy
in blue denim watches oil

spread in phosphorescent scarves
over the cement. He dips
his brush into a bucket and begins

to scrub, making slow circles
and stopping to splash water on the children
who, hours before it opens,

juggle bean bags outside Gantsy's
Ice Cream Parlor,
while they wait for color to drench their tongues,

as I wait for water to bloom
behind me—white foam, as of magnolias,
as of green and yellow

birds bathing in leaves—wait,
as always, for the day, like bread, to rise
and, with movement

imperceptible, accomplish everything.

The House on Main Street

If we had bought the house on Main Street I wanted,
    across from the Shoe Repair Shop
        where the five-bulbed lamp stands
always lit in the window behind the Bilt-rite and Cat's
        Paw signs, I would know now
    who died, know for whom the gray hearse glided

to a delicate stop this morning before the broad red doors
    of the Presbyterian Church, know
        why the whole town was there singing
inside. Where we live on our hill only the deer
        congregate, thin as air, the ghosts
    of lost soldiers, trailing torn flags, as they look

for the deaths they left under the tall pines. But if
    we had bought that house, and could
        begin this day again, then I could early watch
a hundred cars come to town, watch them fill
        the macadam beneath the hoop the town
    kids pound the ball against until their fingers

bleed, cheered on by the Insurance Company's secretary
        and the bevies of pigeons preening
            on the old factory which almost
burned this winter, when Mr. Yeakel's youngest son—who
        thought the town's firemen would surely, if
        they saw him put a fire out, hire him—set

fire to the green garage beside it, and then raised
        the alarm, as alarms were raised
            all year for fires that took stores
and animals, and during the big storm, three
        children's lives. But say again
        that we live on Main Street and it is early

and I can watch the cars pull up beside the charred
        Oldsmobile that still stands where
            the green garage stood, watch the children
poke the bag of clothespins bulging like a wasps' nest
        on the Hanson's umbrella line, watch
        cars block Bridge Street, where, on the steps

of a house the Catholics converted into a church by
        fitting it with green glass and sprinkling
            it with holy water, and which now belongs
to the Mormons, two girls in shorts and lipstick and much-
        arranged hair sit and stare
        at the window behind which the dead man lies. (In whom,

we forget, death has now no interest. But see how
        death is there, touching this man,
            then that, the feathers of a flowered
hat, the preacher's thin hair.) Say I sit
        in our window on Main Street
        and count the people getting out in front

of the latticework propped beside the Shoe Repair Shop
        whose dilapidated face
            made my husband afraid to buy

this house; and say the two fat men who in warm
        weather sun themselves on
    the collapsing porch above the shop come out

with their beer. Say this, for this is why I wanted
        to live here, on Main Street,
        to see what hours those men
like to sit in the sun, to watch down the street
        people passing under the swinging
    tooth-shaped sign and into the dentist's office

of Doctor Joseph Grow, whose beautiful hydrangeas now
        dangle decayed balls over
        the porch rail, to stand
in our yard next to the rusted road sign that points
        West to Portland and the Water
Gap, South to Hope; and this is why I write here

what I write, recalling a funeral to which I was not
        invited, for which the town
        library closed in respect, while
my overdue books sat on the truck's seat and
        baked in the sun that warmed
    that gray hearse, warmed that newly dug hole

in the cemetery, that saw—five years ago among the cedars
        while the cows grazed unperturbed
        in the pines beyond the spear-
barred cemetery rail—a vagrant girl, about
        whom they are now making a movie,
    murdered; the cemetery I stare at so often

from our Bank, watching the small flags flap
        and whistle, watching men
        shovel dirt, watching the keeper
monthly haul dead wreathes and pile them before
        the gate, watching the day
    my daughter and I ran among the stones

with our dog, who rudely peed on many graves, ran there
    together for want of another
        place, in this state where No
Trespassing signs are nailed everywhere, as they were
    not in the wide midwestern
        farmland where I grew up, and one could walk

for miles and miles and never cross a marked fence,
    or hear the heavy tread
        of hunters, or see their bright
guns. It was sunny the day we ran, though
    still winter. It is hard
        to find a home. The earth is not stable beneath

our feet. We slip on the icy grass, our hands
    full of the strange coarsely spotted
        feathers we pick up among
the stones and wish upon, as if by gripping
        them in our palms, or
        stuffing them in our coats, we can be

connected with flight, not with the stone angels
    shadowing the frozen
        ground, but with a body
that has truly flown, with a mind
        that makes the sky
its home.

epilogue

I walk later in the cemetery
to find out who has died, needing to know,
but there are five graves newly filled—
the sweet sour smell of flowers rotting
in their toppled jars heavy on the air.
Alta T. Sprague is here, Frank Hunt, and
Albert Yetter. Under a carved lamb
lies good Earnest Rea; and at the feet

of Ellen T., whose last name is hidden
by a styrofoam Virgin stuck with red
and white carnations and bound by wire
to her marble stone, a bright flag flaps.
These at least are in their graves, unlike
the animals supposedly buried in
our famous pet cemetery which, it turns out,
were never under their fancy markers at all
but had been thrown behind the lake
into huge pits that poisoned all the wells
along Willow Run with their decay.
It grows warm then cold. Along the roads
possums fall beneath our tires. Some years
are years for dying, as they are for fire.

AUGUST KLEINZAHLER

November in West New York

Roofer looks out on the street
flipping his knife
how the Cuban salesman showed him.
You just press the release
and snap your wrist.
Here, try it.
No, not like that, like this.

The street's three maples
are nearly stripped
of the yellow flecking tenement brick
but no storm yet.
Just a soft slow afternoon
on 52nd street.

He's waiting on the storm
and two fat bids.
—One good fucking storm
with lots of wind.
And hail.
And destruction, he says

flipping that blade,
waiting for the phone to ring.

Poetics

I have loved the air outside Shop-Rite Liquor
on summer evenings
better than the Marin hills at dusk
lavender and gold
stretching miles to the sea.

At the junction, up from the synagogue
a weeknight, necessarily
and with my father—
a sale on German beer.

Air full of living dust:
bus exhaust, air-borne grains of pizza crust
wounded crystals
appearing, disappearing
among streetlights and unsuccessful neon.

Storm over Hackensack

This angry bruise about to burst
on City Hall
will spend itself fast
so fluid and heat may build again.

But for a moment the light
downtown
          belongs someplace else,
not here
or any town close.

Look at the shoppers, how palpable
and bright
against gathering dark
like storied figures in stereoscope.

This is the gods' perpetual light:
    clarity
    jeopardy
          change.

Canada Geese in New Jersey

                            Headed north
on the sodded-over trolley track
to Cotysville
            or until carbons blew free
of the brain-stem, out
both ears, settling like soot on wet grass

I heard a honk and made to duck
but two geese slanted past—
getting the hell out of here,
honking all night up the Hudson Valley.

Just like that: *honkhonk:*
a honk about as straight as their necks.
Two big geese can scare up the dead.
Then they're gone.

                  Azalea blossoms stir,
like so many tiny nightgowns.

On the Way Home to Jersey One Night

The same sad stories whip around
and around
streaking the air between dark buildings,
breaking apart in the updraft.

A million tough chances
and Dina's bad back—
galaxies, nebulae of tired old destinies
flying apart in the wind:

the wind off the Hudson,
wrapping itself round the Hotel New Yorker,
riding the aluminum twigs
of a cyclone fence—

something about the wind,
how it roots around in the passageways and lots,
a kind of animal;
and in the night itself,

so dark,
as if everything had been washed out of it—
absence, a terrible absence,
like space.

And the two guys from Chicago,
Algren and Farrell—
I'm always imagining them out there—
in the shadows and doorways,

at every window and busted skylight,
keeping the ledger,

taking the last soiled scraps of it in.

JOEL LEWIS

Pushing the Envelope

The faulty neon of our local
Szechuan takeout puts hairy
lines through the tight, serious
forehead of Dan Rather
& when I look out the window
to vent silent wrath,
all I see are six of a family named
Liu frantically serving Hoboken's
sneakered gringos.

The air feels indispensable
& middle-period Coltrane illuminates the dark
patches of the apartment. Guided by the sweet
science of flexible generosity. I give a call
to Bob, old college friend,
who took up the path of the hermit, as in
hermetic, becoming a cipher to us all
in our diminished leftish clan. Hello Bob,
this is a narrative's worth of old school chums.
We were too young to be hippies, too old
for Punk, too ineffectual to be Yuppies
& like participants in a shotgun wedding (say
Tito Puente & Susan Sontag) we are chatting
as if ten years ago was yesterday's wake-up call.
Happily we are still men of resilience, still
anarchists even, though we wonder of the aliases
of our t-shirt intellectual dreams that
foamed forth in that collegiate cafeteria
over urchin's java & donuts in their twilight.

And what of them all: I sometimes wake
in the night thinking where all those
passionately furious voices went, like Carl
whose standard greeting on those often rainy
Preakness Mountain mornings was: "Whatta Day!!
I wouldn't wish this on a Trotskyite!!"
Or Jimbo, the craziest of our Crazy Maoists,
—now on Wall Street, our only homeowner
& back to the genial, beer-quaffing
ex-linebacker I had first met under
the Student Center's message board.

But am I trying too hard to re-enter my world?
These actual events & persons are blueprints
to the structure of a life just as
neat handwriting defeats the strong ego
And all this memory seems a secret language
through which the world pours its
disinformation. So I sit,
nightstyle of the listless & indebted,
looking outside this small city where
tap water tastes like
the old sneakers flung onto wires
by our furtive urban nomads. And still,
the tab still gets called in just as surely
as standard time is abolished under the eyelash
of the File-O-Fax god. Our ancestor
lapses didn't make this world, did they?

I arrived, like I said, in
a blistered, nameless epoch
with no hope for joy's increase
with all of us wandering books walking
some of us coddling eggs at Urban Farms
some coiling out mock revolution beneath
          thundering espresso's fix
some at a record store's hypnotic jag

some leased out to the strains
          of night, out-lasted night.
It seems so easy to get lost
in the sheer brightness of commodities
& their fine-tuned images.
The big code has cracks, still gets filled
          & if the writing's the spot that dates
all this, then a roofless sky will
arrive to cover up my overlapped
gleanings. See all the cities gleaming
in place champagne sunset. Shadows
demand attention. The image
is a Have-a-Hart trap. Which side of the brain
do you wear your heart? Garrulous landscape.
Goodnight Bob—we'll be talking. Bare night clouds
hand out our silent cues, streetlamps at work
to correct the night's mistakes.

Cape May

The cool of pre-rain weather tints the air
& soft breezes jostle shingles on a pink
gingerbread fort on Hughes & Decatur.
The news stays old here on these
latitudes that swing on through Virginia
& so unlike that Jersey we own;
Paterson's stark inattention, Linden's ocean
of refineries & of stoop dwellers
hooting across Hoboken's urban dawn silence. September
here, with the beach people back home
& this "south Cape Isle" returned
to the mix of sadness & intuition
that's a summer town off-season.

The boardwalk arcades empty in morning's
hanging blue & the surf tom-toms
narrow Poverty Beach with each sloppy wave a
bud already to burst. Up Ocean Avenue is
Victorian cold focus—Our guidebook's #2A:
The Seaview House, once the "thumbprint" cottage
of one Evan Morris. From a builder's illustrated
catalog the proper Victorian could keep up
with his neighbors through a mix 'n match
of carved balconies, elaborate spandrels
& rooster-comb Acroterions. Now listen to
the creaking from massed rocking chairs
on the Chalfonte Hotel's veranda, the Summer draining
with each strolling couple.

The gaslight streets of the historic East End
have been carefully restored to the epoch
of imaginary childhood sing-a-longs
'round the Mason & Hamlin. Here, as
adults, we can imagine our dear phantom
Victorian predecessors arriving by Pennsy's Seashore line
for another season of communal dining
& formal conversation. So, enjoy your illusions
& be an envious ghost in this world of genteel
summer pleasures. Simply count the gables
as you stroll along Corgie Street just as the sun
gets sucked under Delaware Bay, leaving only
gaslight to read the half-moon's script.

                    *   *   *

Sunset Beach is someone's attempt at art photography.
—A black handbook of waves pounds the breakwater
& as all signs on Sunset Blvd. declare,
"Sunken Ship" remains wrecked offshore
—the Atlantus, a prototype concrete ship built during
the steel shortage of WWI. And within site of this barnacle
motel, my wife of one year & I join a clump
of rainy-day sandhogs for a morning of prospecting
for Cape May Diamonds. Though newspapers may have tried

to sell us moonscapes, here we are—picking
milk-white drops from a crumbling shore.

And, perhaps, there are many kinds of stuff
in the concerns of life &, perhaps, empty effort,
that drama of the non-commodity, is one edge
of the daily connection. But the hailing frequencies
of my mind's lining blend in with
a million disparate possibilities & then only one, you
now against the windows of my eyes as our
forgotten instants return to spiral between us
as we watch the whole Atlantic spread out before us
in order to sleep, at sunset's bell.

Why I Am Not a Buddhist

Just before I left for Boulder
I stopped in to see Betty & Jeffery
at *J. Israel Paints* (of which they are
proprietors) to say Goodbye, etc.
I saw Jeff behind the counter
trying to sell peach-white wallpaper
to fat woman with a wart on her lip
that resembled a Japanese Beetle.
            "Where's Betty," I asked
as my eyes surveyed a kingdom of putty knives.
"She's off at a retreat with Swami Muktananda,"
he says. ". . . isn't he the Mick Jagger
among gurus," I inquire. 'You Got IT!"
I flash to when we all three went to
the Yeshiva of Hudson County, reading
Chumash together. Later, Jeff drives me into
Manhattan on the way to the Zendo on West 86th.

Mike was an altar boy
at Our Lady of Fatima. When he was a freshman
at William Paterson, he dropped in for early mass
in the Paterson Cathedral. Although now priding himself
as being an Orthodox Rationalist, he will,
on special occasion, admit to the existence
of a higher being.

I once knew a woman who couldn't make love if there
wasn't a crucifix hanging above the bed & when I visited
Al at the mental hospital, he introduced me
to his hallmate, who, beyond urinating
upon Hackensack bar tops, was convinced
she was carrying the Christ-child full-term.

Jimbo was such a dedicated Maoist that he used to
wake me at 4 am to discuss Lenin's disagreements
with "that renegade Kautsky." On Saturdays,
he took to Paterson's scared streets to sell
copies of REVOLUTION!!, headlines always
in three-inch crimson letters.

—His miraculous ability to survive a Volkswagen's
triple-somersault on a rain-waxed Jersey Turnpike
changed his world-view considerably. He's married now,
works for IBM and watches tv.

Maryanne formed the Atheist's Association with
intentions to drive the born-again Christians
off campus. The group's motto—
We're Atheists—We don't believe in Zeus
& nailed to oak office door
was the statement of principles:
"Atheists have no invisible means of support."
The Orthodox kids in the old neighborhood
put me down for being "too goyish"
and the Catholic School kids beat me up

for "killing their God."
At Boulder's uptown Metaphysical Bookshop
there's a sign hanging: *Shoplifters—*
Remember Your Karma.

It's a sunny day out here in Gregory Canyon,
thanks to somebody or something, powder-blue
butterflies dance around my Ezersoles
while I sit on this marbled rock and peel
a Rocky Mountain Oyster with my Swiss Navy Knife.

May 1981

Hoboken in Advance of the Sunset

Needless and undefined dimensions
limn my walk, of jazz's intuitive process
and the voluptuous latitudes that name a city.
The ancient air flails above my head,
& the menu of Washington Street seems a utopia
of muscular boys, aged young mothers,
and one old German bakery
still absorbing City Hall's whale
in its strudel-full panes.

The quiet tension of massed isolation
plays against the slanting presence
of late afternoon light. The streetlights
change in chronic order and a blue Domino pizza wagon
burns rubber out towards the lowlands of Frank Sinatra Drive
as my thoughts swerve towards
my funhouse reflection in an old woman's glasses.
A mind sets up its scenery, memory dubs in the dialogue,

the city goes outside its history, its soundtrack
within the radios of a teenaged nation.

The resurfaced brownstones are walls of origin
and entry. And behind their walls: a river—
organized water with one idea. Twilight creeps
above the Yardley's neon, boosted
by Linden's fierce petroleum sirocco. We
like it like that. I arrive to
listen. The reticent world's sense of the fabulous.

Main Street, Hackensack

You can no longer tell the pigeons from
the off-river breeze. This twilight factory, streets
as convents, with one lightbulb in an upstairs office
fracturing the black Ad Reinhardt tableau
and though I can recognize the neighborhood,
this Hackensack in Reagan's final year,
I can't be the t-shirt existentialist I once was,
graphing the decline of the empty urban picket.
The county dome's gold glow mimics Washington's skull.
The Woolworth is universal F. W. Woolworth.
And that's a submarine, the S. S. Ling,
moored like a paperweight between the newsprint plant
and the Court Street Bridge.

This all goes into a collective call towards charged silence
that's only cars drifting through amber signals
and buses idling against the Transfer Station platform.
A thick goodbye to the once was,
of Hackensack Saturdays with farmers swarming off up-county's
Susquehanna—those Wortendyke Dutch

and moody Paramus celery ranchers have left their progeny
a vast Mall to inhabit, those lives full-formed
from a violent media's left-over alphabet
of Brand Name Realism.

But you do know that, underneath it all, nothing sits
still, not even here on asphalt
gnawed by sharp-toothed time. Shake pocket change
to realize that oblivion seems miles
and, yet, seconds from the security gates
binding these chilled store fronts.
Each curb a sinking world, each
cataract streetlamp brings up small practical dreams
that illuminate them quickly.

GERALDINE C. LITTLE

Early Spring in the Pine Barrens, New Jersey

Tentative syllables of green. I think
　　how the whole story will unfold, think
how the pitcher plant I canoe towards
　　in its room beneath canes of wild blueberry, net-
work of worts, will speak the climax in midsummer;
　　how oaks will carry on and on, defying
denouement, the blank page after "The End."

Why is my father standing in the canoe
　　like Jesus on his lake of lilies & listeners?
Father in his tomb of bones whole books
　　ago? Summoned by green and words, Irish
father, preacher who wrote God on primroses
　　and nettles, first chapter to last of his life.
Pitcher, preacher; words blend in the content

of this boat illustrated now by sun, birds
　　shuttling over, shadows of worlds resurrected,
and me learning to speak again the litany
　　hanging here like mists of his old land tangled
in subterranean roots to this old land.
　　No monks in monasteries need translate, or tribal
chiefs: *earth, air, fire, water*—

writing to rock any boat, and do.

The Speech of Soil: Homage to Walt Whitman

"Underfoot the divine soil, overhead the sun"
                    —Walt Whitman, "Starting from Paumanok"

Ordinary. You barely notice me under your foot.
Only my absence would shiver your careless stride.
In me rock, mineral particles all
sizes mix with living things, their remains.
I am colorblind: in Georgia maroon as a perfect
claret, in North Dakota intricate nuances
of black. On the beach, holding reflections of birds
and you roaming its reaches for driftwood or renewal
of soul, or stretched on a blanket with lover or child,
I am white, easing silently towards the sea.

At once, I am womb and tomb. This is the message:
they are one. Out of me as I speak
the daisy, complex beyond saying, tilts tendrils
towards light, its roots flesh of your dear dead,
hallowed substance which will receive once more
elements they took (too casually?) on skins you knew—
impulses of moon, stars, sun, wind
with its celebration of the globe's dialects, elegant
fabrics of snow, rain. I hold your tears,
transform them, again and again, into eye's vision.

On me rests what you share world with, weighty
step of a water buffalo in China, graceful
gait of a gazelle approaching a pool in Africa,
singular imprint of a heron adroit on one leg,
ponderous shuffle of a giant tortoise on an island
remote, rare, tremor of the spider's eight toes,
fragile, immense, reverberations still
of creatures held in the memory bank I am

that have spun in the sun their day and passed like the passenger
pigeon. I am their enrichment, an offering to you.

I can distinguish, I tell you I can, the tentative
touch of Eve's naked foot from the sandaled meditation
of Sophocles' step, or the throbbing, merry
movement of Shakespeare's quickening me. I hold as treasure
trudge of a coolie in China, the chained inching
of a black in early America. No footfall is lost;
each is sacred, a pitch in the universe. Listen.
This is the dream and the reality of
a man in love with all there is that we know,
whose passage over me, vibrating hugely, stays.

Mary Ludwig in Old Age

(WHOM HISTORY KNOWS AS MOLLY PITCHER)

Once a year, like returning leaves, they come,
forty green dollars from the Government. My hands,
no longer steady, clutch them: food, heat,

light for the small world of my room. I pay
them out slowly, slowly. A jay shrieks at the window,
raucous, brilliant. *Why do you hoard*, I believe

he scolds. *At your age, be warm, eat well.* He doesn't
yet know how age devours courage and heaven
is a country I can't believe, though I want to, have

always wanted to. Look, if you've seen war,
seen boys spill on the land like a legacy
for worms, you want to believe they've gone to God.

Nights, sometimes, I take a tot of whiskey,
neat. (Oh, never mind pointing the finger,
you in your warm mantle of youth). Before

my scant fire the mind plays tricks with time. I
am as young as you, just married. I see
the beautiful arc of his body over me, hear

lovewords no lady should know, that I *loved*. We
whir to an island dotted with birds—maroon,
jade, cream. They sing us to the only heaven

I *know* exists. Then we all explode, he,
I, birds, island, in an iridescent
flash. We sleep. Everything's right in our world.

Hell. I believe in *that*. At Monmouth, the heat
sucked wits and marrow. What was it all *about*,
anyway? Revolution? *Was anything worth the dying?*

Maggots in boyish flesh move through my dreams
still. And blood, carpeting greeny June
too richly. Johnny, Johnny, I screeched when he fell,

and sprang to his gun. Without thinking. Burning, Furious.
For Johnny. I began to understand something
of how war invades bones like a madness. My hands

on the gun. God! It was power, kicking, whining, flaming.
Beyond anything known. Yes, I ferried pitchers
of water, heart cracking at how those boys panted,

sweat rushing down blackened limbs. Yes.
I did that, couldn't do enough. But the gun.
In my hands . . . I aimed to kill. And make no apology

for it. A demon took over my body. War
at the moment excites while it damns. (*That's* the hell).
After, you weep in the gardens of bones, weep

that you could have planted some of them there (what matter
what side, what color the uniform), weep for what
you'd become. . . . Then it was over. But it is never

over. My mind like a sleeping monster wakes up
when I most want peace, I, an old woman watching
leaves come and go, faster, faster each year,

who would like to think only of how it was when he came
to me first in the high hard bed, how his hand
round a cup of tea in the kitchen was tawny, and kind.

Illuminated Page: Kellsian Fragment in the Pine Barrens of New Jersey

The creek
speaks quietly beside
a silence lovely brimmed
with just belief, that creed
trembling on the tendril
splashing up from weeds
and greenly reaching.

I am moved to an assumption
of the daily bones and beads
of one scribe working
to set down the way it was,
am here to write

whatever sense may seep
into tendons untangling
from overshout and kill.
The swathe of scene before,
around, me, is the margin
everything illumines.

My time here's too little
to understand the squirrel's
astonishing wingless flight,
his centuries' spring and hover
there on a twig of pitch pine.
Or bluejays, bluebells, sounding
like saintly hours
on the stare of frogs—
names of all the world
we know, held, still.

I think how the monk's
habit itchy with lice
and probably lust
held him to a discipline
of doves and gaudy riot
running round luxurious,
and paradoxical, trappings
of God. Matthew, John.
The Christ Himself luminously
sad, the scintillating
cross . . . Look, a human
hand's more comfortable with
less blinding visions. I think
the singing knots and links
caught in Kells,
the skittery wild and somehow
tamed yet never tamed
woodfey, bogshy creatures
were divined as dance,
wine-inspired dreams in blood

too stately wedded, bedazzled
by spring's annunciations
and splendid blasphemies.

Now on my page a heron
drifts its shadow riffled
by wind, like the wing
of a god crossing, recrossing,
blurring distinctions, the weather
of something a man simply
scribing his life fired
into mine trying to find
an essential minimum.

The base metal must be
an assumption of faith.

DOUGHTRY LONG

In Jersey

clocks shake plastic dice
against the morning's ear
streets gyrate a holy-ghost coma
incorrect history puts its afro on
ready to enter center stage
we rush step on to cables
turn back our tribes
the cycle sucks africa from us
we collect second prizes
soul of gold
prophets dressed in ego-mythologies
come to explain new crosses
elipse sana mo tana zaba
elipse sana mo tana zaba
they repeat
words that will not break the mourning
the mail arrives on nerve ends
revolutions arrive
holding their wrists
complaining about violence in the streets
hate, an equator of sun
and the radio says that the world is ending
but that the weather will be fair tomorrow

Untitled

No one lives in Trenton after 3:30 in the morning
except street walkers, the groaning pendulum of factories
and certain ghosts who question
why they have returned

At Fitz's Place

music pours perfect wine from the juke-box
couples turn tomorrows and yesterdays
over in their glasses
    time straight up
    history on the rocks
    dreams with just a twist,
overhead ceiling fans spin flashes of blurred conversation
perfumed women curled and shined flash jewels in their smiles
men sugar-coat the moment,
it's Friday night in Trenton
the last days of a fleeting summer,
    to want more
    to be more
    to do more,
we sit watching
involved in knowing too that there is something more
it will take almost forever before things will be as they were,
outside, the night air lifts us above the moment
above the city.
    we long for love when we are children
    we long for God when we grow older and
    this is all that there is
    but there's so much more.

PABLO MEDINA

October

I walk into a field of cat grass and weeds,
clumps of trees, rubble.
I people the field with memories of ancient wars,
focus on a peasant with a club foot walking home.

I think of someone who came to me
in a dream hoping to start over
and I was cold like the wind that rips
across the flatlands bringing snow
and its silence, a tuft or two
of grass sticking through the ice.

The field is in New Jersey. There are no peasants
here; no battle-weary ghosts rise from the ground.
There is a face I can barely remember.

Miles away on the right factories belch their smoke
and a steel bridge carries trucks over a channel.
They say the field stretches to the sea and almost
touches the waves. I cannot see that far.

View Downriver

That bridge is a poem
he said donning his jacket
as the wind whipped up the leaves.

Trenton makes.

The world
doesn't know beauty.
The river shows its teeth
ready to swallow children.

Takes
a blind eye,
a man
ready to drop at the factory door.
Balls it's cold he said.

Takes knowing
what those letters say,

a few beers
not to see the bed at night,
the wife spread open
like a crusty beach,
daughters polishing their nails
laughing at his pitted teeth.

Takes giving up,
a chance to die in peace.
No questions asked.

6:40 to Trenton

All these people, trains,
evening papers, flapping ties.
All this longing for a kiss
in the darkness, flicker of candle tongue.

Rain dances in the clouds,
music drops on the arcing ground
at the end of the ride.

All the courage to swim wide flesh,
to enter the eyelid of a dream,
the country where the elements of loss
are small black birds
disappearing into blue.

Sam's Deli, South Broad

The tall man with the hair
cut straight across the forehead
lounges smoking cigarettes.

You don't even get a napkin
with your hamburger.

I remember a girl long ago
I made love to with my socks on.

Some twist of life
brought Sam, bristled and chubby,
to this landmark of grease
in the gut of Trenton.

The tall man asks for a Klondike
bar, then the usual for lunch.

I remember the bitter cold outside
and her gasps like a bellows on the couch.

A cat drifts among styrofoam towers.
Love was surrender then, and now

South Broad, no napkin, ketchup
dripping out of the bun.

State Complex

Steeples rise with chimneys and bureaucracies
to dim the sun. The river is forgotten, horizontal.
The city lavishes upon itself the clarity of numbers.
The temples resemble offices, the offices
resemble prisons, the prisons resemble factories.
After all these years and marble steps
only the river knows where it goes.
Or cares not following the pull of accidence.

In the park I think of ancient Chinese poets
so distant from the stains of history.
They knew their fallacies and drank their wine
while winds wore pavilions down to stone
and scattered the imperial dreams of permanence
they celebrated.

Wisp of death. Ripple of rapids and curve of light
over the bank. At dusk the weeds and garbage
gain distinction. The structures hum in Sunday rest,
yellow like urine or gold. God a huge cat slinks
through parking lots and autumn strokes the avenues.
It is cold. The night pours out like water.

JOYCE CAROL OATES

The Present Tense

in which I live hurtles airless a razor's swift slash
so deep there is no blood for the first instant no pain
except to the brain's eye the present tense is crammed
with fictitious memories curling snapshots in albums
the cheerful pretense of a history shared as we share stanzas
of coy old love songs no one ever sings

the present tense in which I live is a morning of Canada geese
passing overhead in their uncanny formations crying to one
    another
in a language I can't decode and the single deer bounding
through our woods graceful as if this were the Morning of
    Creation
the present tense is a telephone ringing and a stranger's raw voice
Who is that? and my own *Who is that?*—the Sand-Man on
    his way,
a husband I never married—and then the dial tone the seamless
present tense

it might be called a rosary as the moments slip by smooth
as beads worn by ancient fingers smooth as flimsy prayers
that rise to the lips in numbed panic or in comfortable routine
though just as reasonably it is the frantic buzz of a wasp trapped
between windows or in the skull or yawning in the
    daffodil-bright
sunshine or whispering psalms in honor of the dead

it is embraces and Valentine kisses and a soul small enough
to be carried in a spoon it is gaily aswarm with flying seeds

in celebration of those sequoias that live forever but are only
legends in this part of the world it might be that drawer
of snarled string and loose nails and the cats' matted hairbrush
it makes the charge *Now the day is passing, now the day is gone,*
what did the day mean, why did you see so little—

the present tense in which I live hurtles airless you forget
you haven't breathed for minutes a Chopin cadenza too swift
to be heard the birds startling up from the ledge in an explosion
of sleek grackle wings the present tense flies overhead too swift
to be grammatical it is all one stammered syllable shared
as we share songs we never sing it is all we know
it might be heaven, or hell,
or all we know

Dreaming America

for my mother, Carolina Oates

When the two-lane highway was widened
the animals retreated.
Skunks, raccoons, rabbits,—even their small corpses
were transformed into rags
and then into designs
and then into stains
then nothing.

When the highway was linked to another
and to another
six lanes, then nine, then twelve arose
sweeping nobly to the horizon
along measured white lines.
The polled Herefords were sold.
The barbed-wire fences dismantled.

When the cornfields were bulldozed
the farmhouses turned to shanties;
the barns fell;
the silos collapsed.

When the fields were paved over
Frisch's Big Boy reared seventy feet in the air.
Sunoco and *Texaco* and *Gulf* signs gaily competed
on hundred-foot stilts.
Eyeballs on stalks:
miraculous!
And illuminated all night.

Where that useless stretch of poplars lay
an orange sphere of gigantic proportions
announces *Wonderland East*, open
for Thursday evening shopping.
Here, tonight, packs of teenagers hunt
one another.
The terrazzo footprints are known by heart.

Where did the country go?—cry the travelers, soaring
past. *Where did the country go?*—ask the strangers.
The teenagers never ask.

Where sway-backed horses once grazed in a dream that had
    no history,
tonight a thirteen-year-old girl stands dreaming
into the window of Levitz's Records & Hi-Fi Equipment.
We drive past, our speed accelerating. We disappear.
We return.

F———

for Robert Phillips

If you stare long enough it becomes beautiful.
O look: if you translate its *colors* into comely *sounds*:
ochre, russet, coppery-pink, nutmeg.
Soon it is an anti-world,
another way of seeing.

An industrial slum gaily glaring in a midsummer squall.
Your car slows, you are hypnotized, the sickly air has trapped you.
How porous smoke rises heavy and leaden-pale as a giant's
      thigh,
how the air heaves visibly in gusts,
sulphurous peonies blooming in the wind.
Here, an ancient sea-bed
guarded by a fifteen-foot Hercules fence.
Clouds break companionably about the highest smokestacks.
There is no amazement to the factory windows, opaque with grime,
as they slant open into the 100° shade.

What is there to say about these regions of our earth,
these domestic hells, these landscapes familiar
as high-tension wires whining overhead,
throbbing power on all sides?
Scars' stitchings in the earth. Miracle rainbows in the air.
What is there to say, why the wish to interpret,
to make judgments,
to record a vision?

If you stare long enough it translates into language.
The base of the pyramid—of course.
The history of labor in North America, the billyclubs, the militia,

the Pinkerton's men, the slaughter, the bleeding eyes, the
    barbed wire.
This is the base of the pyramid as always but it is not strewn
    with workers' bones.
It glowers and winks instead with their acres of parked cars.

O acres, acres!—acres of parked cars. And all American,
and all very new.

Is the air noxious?—but you are the one who has weakened.

You are the one who ponders, which creatures graze in these
    pastures,
which monsters brood beside such rancid ponds—
mutant fish, giant crab-spiders of wire and rust,
toads with swollen white bellies,
armored things with spiny tails and eyes that stare unmoved
from the tops of stalks.

You are the sole observer to see *Ford* wittily obscured by grime,
to *F——*.
You are the only eye to record a plastic wreath at the top
of the highest smokestack, which you have been seeing for
    months:
Joy to the World   Gilmore Chemicals

Or is it another anti-world,
another way of seeing?

Leavetaking, at Dusk

The house is empty, nearly.
It thinks nothing now, it has given away its secrets
cheaply.

Room after room,
the blankness of walls
we have not seen before.
Bare hardwood floors. Geometrical precision.
Dusk flattened like a stranger's face
against the north windows.

The house is no one's now,
it is nothing human.
A past and a future, but no present.

We pass through it, invisible.
Now the ceilings rise.
A lone mad cricket sings in a corner.

Another

Another dusk: coldly whitely blue,
and the great spruces humbled with snow,
again the western distance bruised with sun,
again the stillness seeping
out of the earth's core.

Another dusk, and it is that moment
when the heart falters at such beauty—
though isn't it routine,
smug as clockwork?
Why must you interpret everything as a sign?
As if you wanted to be injured!

Another dusk: deepening now into night,
and again the reflection in the window
floating in the mock depth of the glass,
taking ghost-colors out of the night.

Yes—another dusk, and why
must you stare melancholy and smiling?—
as if everything were new,
as if night had no history,
and that woman's face in the window,
so suddenly visible, a baptism
into a prodigious self.

Another dusk: deepening into night.

ALICIA SUSKIN OSTRIKER

In the Autumn of My Thirty-Seventh Birthday

Going to work
on the bus
      —Needles strike
the window, O it's gonna be a cold rain
    says an old woman.
        *

Leave dreary desk
take walk on dreary campus
    within his bending sickle's compass come
      seed pods
    brown hard durable
I collect them
        and recall
      the pulse, desire and flight of a drift
        of timorous cherry blossoms
          outside my house
            an age ago, last spring:
Must I go, then?
Must I learn to crawl naked into the cold?
        *

In the afternoon on the bus
schoolgirls are flirting and shrieking.
    Their glow
    does not concern them
      but penetrates through bus walls and
      hurtles for miles through the wet Jersey woods

as we drive past the graveyard
and then past houses
where they live and yelling one by one get off.

*

Slick Joni Mitchell
on the record player
spaghetti and meatballs
salad ice cream
Gabriel's laughter
Rebecca's hair
Eve's hazel eyes
J's victory at squash
William Carlos Williams dancing nude
nothing to me, nothing, nothing.
It is right here, the hole
no good thing fills.

*

Behind me there is an eye
of a mysterious monster
says Gabriel
but when I turn around
it hides
             (we riding bike
             up to Jack & Jill
             for extra sweets)
         and while he hugs me
             the pumpkins rot
             in the fields

*

12:30 a.m.
J. like a pod next to me
I want to sleep, I want my healing dreams

Long conversation with N. just divorced
her shrink tells her to take

anti-depressant pills
she doesn't want to
her shrink says she'll be a winning horse
she doesn't want to—
what does she want? to die?

Gabriel howling
off and on like a light bulb
   or a dark bulb - confused - like rushing
      winds, branches thwarting branches
         he calls, and cannot stop.
I go to him.

The Raven of Death

A grey November morning. We make love
On our old marriage bed, strong, sweet.

Without a sound, the raven of death
Passes between us a black, serrated wing.

Across the long fields of Jersey and Pennsylvania
Corn stands in yellowed rows.

We are perspiring, pressing together. The raven
Softly lifts to a black dot in the sky.

The Leaf Pile

Now here is a typical children's story
that happens in gorgeous October

when the mothers are coming
in the afternoon, wearing brisk boots
and windy skirts to pick up
the little children from the day care center

Frost in the air
the maples golden and crimson
my son in a leaf pile in the playground dreaming
I am late, the playground is almost
empty, my husband will kill me

I gather my son to go home,
he forgets his sweater in the playground and I send him back
he dawdles, he is playing with leaves
in his mind, it is already a quarter
to six, will you come on I say

and hurry along the corridor, there are yellow and blue rocket
paintings, but I feel bad and ask what did you do today,
do you recognize this story, the way he stands and picks
his nose, move I say, do you want dinner or not
I'm going to make a nice dinner, fried chicken

I wheedle, so could you please walk a little
faster, okay, I walk a little faster and get upstairs
myself, pivot on boot-heel, nobody there,
he is putting something in his mouth, his sable eyelashes
downcast, and I am swooping down the stairwell screaming

> damn you
> that's filthy
> I told you not before dinner

We are climbing the stairs
and I am crying, my son is not crying
I have shaken him, I have pried the sweet from his cheek
I have slapped his cheek like a woman slapping a carpet
with all my strength

mothers are very strong
he is too young to do anything about this
will not remember he remembers it

The mind is a leaf pile where you can bury
anything, pain, the image of a woman
who wears a necklace of skulls, a screaming woman
you dig quickly and deposit the pulpy thing
you drop leaves on it and it stays there, that is the story

that is sticking in my mind as we push
the exit door, and run through the evening wind
to my car where I jerk the gearshift and pick
up a little speed, going along
this neat suburban avenue full of maples
the mark of my hand a blush on my son's cheek.

Beer

After the store and the gas station close
There is still the bar,
With its real animal heads on the wall
Alert and thoughtful under their antlers,
Neither refusing nor rebuking you,
Its television they have tucked
Under the ceiling
Like a man holding a pingpong ball under his chin,
Where it yammers like a nervous female
Who uses her hands
More than a person needs to.

Your neighbors will be playing pool, sadly
And easily as they always do,
The teenage women hyped-up, more serious

Than their boyfriends,
The drunkards loud and wide
Like semis cruising down the interstate,
Their bellies stacked, a proud, rounded
Lifetime record of beer to show,
The snaky boys keeping their angular
Mouths shut, chalking their cues.

It could be raining or snowing outside.
Night after night somebody puts
"You Can Take This Job and Shove It"
On the jukebox, and you can hardly help
Loving the familiar bodies, the sounds,
The movements, and how everything goes together
For hours.

Surviving

*Soon the time will come when I don't
have to be ashamed and keep quiet
but feel with pride that I am a painter.*
*—Paula Modersöhn-Becker
to her mother, July 1902*

*We meant while we were together to create
A larger permanence, as lovers do,
Of perfecting selves: I would imitate
By my perfections, yours; I would love you
As you me, each to the other a gate.*
—Marie Ponsot, "Late"

i
It is true that in this century
To survive is to be ashamed.

We want to lie down in the unmarked grave,
We want to feel the policeman's club that cracks
A person's head like a honey-melon, and lets
Human life spill like seeds, we want to go up
In milky smoke like a promise.
If we're women it's worse, the lost ones
Leach our strength even when we are dancing,
Crying *no right* under our shoes,
When we are working, there is that nameless weariness:
Lie down, lie down, a mule in a dusty ditch
The cart shattered into boards—
Who can urge us to pull ourselves onward?
How can the broken mothers teach us?

It is true that when I encounter another
Story of a woman artist, a woman thinker
Who died in childbirth, I want to topple over
Sobbing, tearing my clothing.

ii

A painting of a peasant woman's hands
As strong as planks, influenced by Cezanne
Who had struck her "like a thunderstorm, a great event,"
That first visit from Germany to Paris.
She was a raw girl, then,
But the thought was clear.
A coarse canvas of an orange, a lemon,
Local deep-red tomatoes, two Fauve asters,
Globes and rays,
Designed like a reclining cross.
A naked woman and baby painted curled
On a mat, lacking a blanket, a portrait
Of what all skin remembers
And forgets.
I walked from painting to painting. I watched this woman's
Earth pigments growing thicker, more free,
More experimental,
Force augmented, it seemed, every year.

"The strength with which a subject
Is grasped, that's the beauty of art"
She wrote in her diary.
And she had resisted the marriage to Otto,
Had wished to remain in Paris
Painting like a Parisian, a modernist
But he had begged.
When they returned home, she knew herself
Already pregnant, delighted with pregnancy.

iii

(1876–1907)
The little cards on the gallery wall
Explained the story.
Language is a form of malice.
Language declares: *Here is a dead thing.*
I cover it over with my thin blanket.
And here is another dead thing.
Please to notice, you soon can feel
Nothing. Not true. Although I did not
Fall, I could feel the heart
Attack, as she rose from childbed, the beleaguered
Grief, in my chest and womb,
That throttled cry, nature is not our enemy,
Or the enemy is also the ally,
The father, the mother,
The powerful helpless hills
Where the pigment comes from.

iv

Only the paintings were not elegiac.
The paintings, survivors
Without malice—can it be?
Squeezed into me like a crowd
Into an elevator
At nine A.M. Pressing against each other,
Carrying their briefcases in one hand,

Pushing my buttons with the other,
Go ahead up, they said,
You have no choice.

Carry us to our floors, our destinations,
Smoothly if you will, do not break down.
On the first floor
When the doors slid open
A child rested her chin on a city stoop
Among the giants.
There were many such scenes, viewed briefly.
At the forty-sixth floor, before
The doors could close, my mother
Rushed inside, carrying her shopping bags
And wearing her scuffed loafers.
Alone in the elevator
At the mercy of the elevator
So much space around her,
Four plans of polished aluminum,
Such indirect lighting,
Such clean and grinning chrome.
An entire blankness
And she was trusting it
To bear her down,
And she was talking, talking.

v

Today I got a big bargain
In chickens, she says, and a pretty big bargain
In skim milk. Skim milk's bluish
Like mother's milk. Did I ever tell you
I fought the doctors and nurses
The very day you were born. They said
"You'll stick a bottle in her mouth"
But I nursed you, I showed
Them. And did I tell you
When I was hungry because your father

Didn't have a job, I used to feed you
That expensive beef puree, spoonful by spoonful
Until you would throw up,
And then I would feed you a certain amount
More to make sure you were full
Although I was starving.
Did I tell you that one.

Mother, a hundred times.

Did I tell you I was president
Of the literary society
When your father met me.
Did I say that he called me "Beatrice of the beautiful eyes."
Did I tell you about the prize
I won for my poems.
Yes.

The checkout girl at the Shoprite
Tried to cheat me
Today but I caught her.
I told George but he was watching television.
He never pays attention, he pretends
He's deaf. Would you phone me
Saturday.

vi

So my mother should have been a writer. Her mother,
A Russian beauty, should have been a singer.
"She lost the bloom of her youth in the factories,"
My mother says, a formula sentence she is obviously
Repeating, and her eyes fill up like paper cups.
It is seventy years later. Explain these tears.

No promise of help or safety, every promise of cruelty,
Impoverishment, that is our world. John Keats loved it,
Coughing bright red. Hart Crane, also, sank into it,
Like a penny the pig-white passenger throws

Into the water to watch the boys who will
Dive. Explain *St. Agnes' Eve.* Explain *The Bridge.*

Explain these tears.

vii

We are running and skipping the blocks
To the Thomas Jefferson swimming pool
Where we'll both get in free
For the morning session,
You pretending to be my under-twelve
Elf-faced sister, and when we've gone through
The echoing cavernous girls' locker rooms
Where underfed blonds shiver
Knock-kneed as skeletons, the water drops
Standing out on their skin like blisters,
And we're in the water
Green and chlorinous
Cool in the August day
You hug me, mother, and we play
Diving under each other's legs
Until children collect around you like minnows
And you lead us in ring-a-rosy,
You get even the smallest ones to duck
Heads underwater, bubbling and giggling
Don't be afraid! Breathe out like this! Then we all sing
Songs against Hitler and the Japs.
I get to be closest. You're mine, I'm good.
We climb out, dripping on the tiles—
That bright day's faded. Today you are still running
As if you pushed a baby carriage
From a burning neighborhood.

viii

What woman doesn't die in childbirth
What child doesn't murder the mother
The stories are maps to nowhere

ix

A late self-portrait: it's a screen of foliage green
Enough to be purple, and here in front of it
The woman artist, crude, nude to the waist,
Fingers her amber beads, secretly
Smiling, like no man's wife

x

Mother my poet, tiny harmless lady
Sad white-headed one
With your squirrel eyes
Your pleading love-me eyes
I have always loved you
Always dreaded you
And now you are nearly a doll
A little wind-up toy
That marches in a crooked circle
Emitting vibrations and clicks.
Mother, if what is lost
Is lost, there remains the duty
Proper to the survivor.
I ask the noble dead to strengthen me.
Mother, chatterer, I ask you also,
You who poured Tennyson
And Browning into my child ear, and you
Who threw a boxful of papers, your novel,
Down the incinerator
When you moved, when your new husband
Said to take only
What was necessary, and you took
Stacks of magazines, jars
Of buttons, trunks of raggy
Clothing, but not your writing.
Were you ashamed? Don't
Run away, tell me my duty,
I will try not be deaf—
Tell me it is not merely the duty of grief.

Los Angeles, 1977/Princeton, 1985

His Speed and Strength

His speed and strength, which is the strength of ten
years, races me home from the pool.
First I am ahead, Nike, on my bicycle,
no hands, and the *Times* crossword tucked in my rack,
then he is ahead, the Green Hornet,
buzzing up Witherspoon,
flashing around the corner to Nassau Street.

At noon sharp he demonstrated his neat
one-and-a-half flips off the board:
Oh, brave. Did you see me, he wanted to know.
And I doing my backstroke laps was Juno
Oceanus, then for a while I watched some black
and white boys wrestling and joking, teammates, wet
plums and peaches touching each other as if

it is not necessary to make hate,
as if Whitman was right and there is no death.
A big wind at our backs, it is lovely, the maple boughs
ride up and down like ships. Do you mind
if I take off, he says. I'll catch you later,
see you, I shout and wave, as he peels
away, pedalling hard, rocket and pilot.

Some Days in March

March 13. Afternoon.

Sunlight between the blinds
Dust on the pillow
Brahms in the next room
And your hands on me

All were as if some stranger shared the bed
Smiling, and slid a cool blade in my bones.

March 14. Towards Equinox.

After many gray days, and early darkness,
Today, when I leave work, it is still bright,
And I perceive, an instant, as I am running for a bus; between
                                buildings the sun:
Great ruby, dying, dying.

March 15. Morning.

Three seconds after you left, in a brusque
Untoward fit of joy: the coffee? the kiss?
I leapt to the window, to the windowsill's level,
Dragged up the blinds and stood, to catch you, to catch *you*
Who bounded like a fox into the day.

March 16. The Grievance.

Roll out of this bed,
Go sleep in that bed.
Will you waste, for some few
Cold words of mine, one whole
And irrecoverable night, fool?

March 17. A Promise.

Time does not waste me.
If I had nothing
But wine and candles
And your touch at night, my friend,
I would survive forever.

March 18. The Thaw.

A tigerish, unnatural heat.
It makes you want to be poor
And sit on a stoop
In the evening, drinking beer, suffering.
Summer's coming.

March 19. On the Evening Bus.

That young girl with the cornstalk's soul
Is on the bus with me again.
I know her secretly,
How under the awkward (trying to look like the other girls)
Flimflam, she is pale green,
Veined, and with strength.
How she might (will not) might swallow the sun in her beauty
Were she once undressed, with her face washed very clean.

March 20. Frost Again.

The trees are climbing
Over the hill.
The vines are climbing
Over the trees.
They do not breathe.

March 21. Equinox.

All day I could sleep
Until white spiders came
And spun threads between
Finger and finger
And dust settled on my hair
And Spring went away weeping.

James Ruggia

"I woke into another man's day . . ."

I woke into another man's day
& grumbled his opinions over his newspaper
& kissed his wife at the morning door
& the busdriver knew his name & his special
curse for Monday & the waitress knew his eggs
like he likes 'em
& I finally understood the stocks & bonds pages
& could nod confidently at his secretary
& on his desk his wife is sad in the eyes of her photo
& makes me think of all the operations crisscrossing
her belly & in his drawer I find brochures
of bright Miamis
& later I eat his meal & see his reflection
on the microwave oven & watch his children silent
stare, pushing pot roast slow across their plates
into the mush of mashed potatoes
& through his door into the cool evening mist, I kneel
in his knees, look up to where the mute stars
shine & put his face into my opened hands.

Meadowlands

for Tim Daly

From here, distant Newark's toy castle
    towers over the marsh.
Bent girders,
        charred black

& rust-red, writhe
       against the reeds
              leaning under a tumbling wind.
Ruptured auto husks
       shotgun sprayed, rot
   under billboards. Tractor colored
       barrel piles collapse
              & corrode on dead soil.
Herons rise out of reed stands
       send water still circles
              through forests of cat tail
& mouth the sun coppered sky
       past the pumps & dull neons of Vince
Lombardi Service Center
towards an old viaduct's black iron bone.
The dead iron combs
the rune & rubbish laden wind
       for newspapers, breakfast boxes
              & the bright fast food bags
that spell out the language of our land.
Tugs, trucks & hungry
       gulls haul it out where
spiny dogs prowl down deserted dock streets,
their lips on the curl,
       like the man-masks local
              boys make of their faces,
a rage which will
turn in time to eat their minds.

Earth Angel

Within the jagged edges
       of a 60s snapshot
the teen idol

hands in pockets & smokes
        stuffed in his shoulder sleeve,
                leans back in the neon
glow of a window's pulsing PIZZA sign.

Avenue light
moves from those eyes
        on the stride's
                bright Friday.
His smile's shining hood
        rides its chrome indian
                over the line, radio high;
a hard faith
        shining bright on the heart's
                roaring engine
to a stone wall's stop.

Soft siren lights
douse the tree boughs;
        firemen hose the road.

Sparkling shards of glass
glisten in my brother's blood.

An August Dog

Subway lips lick ugly. Taxis launch
against the light,
                turning heads
& spinning swollen fumes
        on the sweating flesh of a staggered
Noon's park bench collapse.

Lanky Rastas hustle bags
to secretaries stuffing their shirts
with laughter.

      The hotdog man stares through pork
      steam, inhales their ha-has,
      a bundle of kraut
          dripping from the fork in his hand.

A sour immigrant's fat
     spouse howls at her dull
          son's baseball boxscores.

Scribbling puns
from Finnegan's Wake
on his Chinese take out carton,
the old scholar stops to stick a snot
from his corned beef nose in my pocket.

"Vanity" he moans. My mentor.

DAVID SHAPIRO

Snow

> At first the snow thawed quietly
> and secretly from within.
> —Pasternak

> On few days has the dark sky cleared.
> —Po Chü-i

Since I was born in the city of Newark
Moment by moment a very fine snow has been falling.
On very few days has it stopped snowing in my sleep.
The snow has widened till it joins the roofs; elevators sink
Into it; in sleep I build snow fortresses.
The sleep I have slept is also snow—
Snow poisonous as underpainting in Spain—
Snow in the surface as wide as an exile—
Snow in the airplanes that almost touch your face—
I advise you not to paint it.
At the end of the street I hear a snowy song;
Snow birds are lost in Chinese white snow;
In a single night parts of the car have turned to snow;
Another car moves forward for science.
Snow has fallen into the old bottle of eraser fluid.

from *Friday Night Quartet*

III. *Orange-Colored Sky*

My mother said,
I couldn't keep my hand off your face,
I was always caressing your chin.
We used to listen to a television program, you and I,

And the guy sang a song called "Orange-colored Sky"
And his name was George. He'd say GEORGE.
So we wrote a letter to him, and I wrote it for you and I said
I am five years old and a classical musician
   who plays the violin

And I really prefer Bach and Beethoven
But I like the way you sing "Orange-colored Sky"
And he read it out loud to all the people in the audience
And you heard it, and he said, "This is a letter from
   a little boy, David Shapiro, Hopson
   Street, Newark," which got a laugh.

Red Boats

We ended up the night searching
searching in a little house & this time
it was my house & he never saw
how we got past the others who
were also lighted up until we got past
your face & we got past your
smoke & then we stood up on it & I saw
a particular face there which was golden, full
of dirt called Paul & this time we were

in the park so naturally he said, The boats
& we went but we were still searching
searching & now his name was Jeff but they
didn't let us on, they didn't give us
a boat. Later,
I found myself on the lake
anyway, drifting toward the bank where all the weeds were
I said Lord I can't see you here
I've stopped reading your book you
only had one bird he kept changing color
even in paradise where
all the great men get together & pity my poems.
Still, we ended up the night
searching, searching
& someone here wants to say Please
but it's hard & someone
wants to tell you the unusual place & you will
die & he wants you to remember him
telling you this
& he wants you to remember him
please, when you see how strange
it is, walking into the
boathouse the lavatory so sweet &
so strange & he wants you to remember
when you look out the window
especially he wants you to remember
yes & watch all the red boats in the sun
before a blossom blows up in your kidneys & you're gone.

A Study of Two Late July Fourths

Now this little boat in hypnosis sets forth
It was a collaboration with cardboard bellman and beaver
    overboard

Giving up the agony of America or concrete rot
Like a realist forced to fix the swiftly falling buildings

This is how one departs from the forest of a drawing
Or tracing
My father the soldier stands upon the rock
Like the *Magnificat* sadly inverted and clinging to the riddle's
    neck

I am playing in my mother's lap
As she reads a book I will never see
My father put money on a house; it collapsed structurally
Give up give up the pavilion of the sun give up

Give up capital gain like capital losses
Capitulate taking it off like a cardigan
As one who hides a Broken Dutchman
In secret disseizin unlimited misgovernment give up the green
    helicopter under green trees

And all this Scotch tape turning color in the blue sun *gibs auf*
Alone and relative like bread and wine
As one decends the escalator to the gods desire and
    representation
And rage: at a humiliating height observe the death of the
    garden

Popeye averted in yellow skiff red bottom green spinach
And pink muscle raised like a toy Liberty
Memory bank, memory drum, memory track, memory switch
And the nymph says No, like sand sinking into oil at sea

Something big is happening to us
And it is driving me to the bottom
I know what washes away and who I am
Love, I am reading your lips

I the poor predictor predicted this catastrophe
Oxymoronic and disheveled the universe in summer pleasure
The eyeglasses look at you like a compact Spanish dictionary
The robot edges toward the conservator

You will sleep on this typewriter like a model prison
Reiterate that we did not kill you
As one who wants to be alone with his laughter
The raped Sabines come back and the rejected parts break
   through

At the edge of a gem
I met you as the object slipped into its own slipstream
Dancers swayed upon the helicopter
Over a broken bridge

The Boy Who Loved Bubbles

Because a universe is one bubble
of black bubbles, and yet
a boy is watching always with bloody eyes
—a boy who loves bubbles—
as a black stone rises beside our sleeping head

Tame at the end of a stem
it may not burst like paper
into fifty sheets
as he knows who stripes his notebook with lithographs
Inserting his pen into his mother's black purse
he covers it he discovers it in a glance
with schedules and weeks and a bitten newspaper
But he is looking for writing, the black bubbles

Now what emerges is the antonym
a clipping as colorful and useless as a singularity

and mother's black planet
Now bubble and syllable break in the evening air

You were not really listening to the last sentence
Because you could not see it, the transparent dump we live in
    like a frothy star
Now you are really listening so I will tell you the end

Inside the bubble is another bubble, of course
Inside the stone is a star of pain

Exploding like an accident, the wild syllable, wet
The king delighted by forbidden hair
Poems of birth that were not poems of birth
Music and panic engendered by a prophet without vision
The nostril of an injured monster flaring with a pill

Toby and Nairobi, Thetis the magician
Stigmata on the wand Difficulties of the stateless A cab ride
    wrong
    A ride home Relays
Reading in the dark nothing but the kaleidoscope of the last
    century

The Destruction of the Bulwarks at Deal

1.

To begin with, my rising with you near the Deal Apartments;
    and my heart, always in ferocious projects, worries you
with distances and dark, with the perishing tendrils
    in your hands still of the absurd, individual gift.

But if I tried to grab the child, this moment he becomes me
    Or to seize you without suffering
my eyes in their skinny gaze hold, cover you no more.

The afternoon stone.
How many, our truest summers gone, the townsmen plundered you
    selfless, dreamless, on the lopsided shore
and you quailed in horror
while the bloated gulls beat past the poles

2.

Lord I sleep and I sleep

I am haunted all night by the look of cars

When I sleep they can speak, they say: Ride me,
    David. I am fast as death

Well who lighted this road up? Who made me this clear?

You know I am soft as plasma

I am haunted by all these things

I am crushed instantly

Deal Winter Composition

dry tongues
    might;

and a slogan
    that nurtures

the sea bird and the
    loser

it shall
        console them

All the gray
        squadrons

of mental
        concretion

the endless
        traffic and

surrender
        of poet

and tendril,
        all the melancholy

congregation
        tracts and domains, expansions,

overheard, or
        partly heard even

it shall
        console them:

a face a glyph
        climbing in the mist

toward you,
        and a long granitic coast

stretched before your thumb your
        eyes, gestures

and groves,
        in a white season.

HERSCHEL SILVERMAN

Brecht West

for Eric Krebs

long-haired granny-glassed bell-bottomed student faces
conversing in old drugstore now converted informal
    coffeehouse,
New Brunswick New Jersey Easton St.
conceived by Eric Krebs, ex-wrestler, student, poet, playwright,
ole-movie promotor of V. Pudovkin, Eisenstein, Hitchcock,
Charley Chaplin—King Kong overlooking neat chairs and
    tables
where sit Rutgers angel-faced students, Douglass English majors
some with accents reminiscent of Oxford put-on,
some non-student poets around to read their poems—
colored strobelites and hi-fi music, massagic—
Viveca Lindfors advertised in One-Woman-Show April 4th
with discussion on arts to follow
i suppose to enhance Brecht West's image—
quiet kissing of ancestral lips and conversation
soft—guitar strumming Folk—
thin girls in jeans, thin-hipped, small breasts
that seem aflame at confessional reading poems of love—
friends at table loudly clapping—
celestial thoughts—
the Easton streetside door slamming to Eternity—
words lost as new heads appear between hanging curtains in
    doorway,
rhythm broken, i pause in midst of nite train poem
to glance toward door then go on reading words
of Coney Island nitemare train of generation Past

to this gathering Now, serious hippie-kids
attired in threads of old fantasy—
my ancient green-couch dreams come true
in poetic pyramid coffee-house labyrinth 1969 Springtime—
Beautiful Pat McCole, blind, listens to poems
in Brecht West this St. Patrick's Day
digging the sounds in tortured mind, acute,
almost ready to nervously recite a poem of own—
funny apology self-consciously made by reader of an obscene word—
a meerschaum professor secret poet admirer sits inhibited
quiet almost hidden in dark corner—
nude art-work hung on walls where previously Ex-lax, alcohol,
fennel tea, and hairpins stood—
in back a bar with coffee urns and old movie memories of Youth—
a ghost rising Christ-like in psychedelic mind
as Mrs. Cotton poem powerfully makes trip from Occult
and Zuber's idiot hungry feeds New Brunswick—

March 17, 1969

May 5, 1979

little black train-engine
brought up from Central America
to Paterson
about as old as my Bayonne townhouse

Paterson once a prosperous powerful city
now growing strong with poetry

old factories near Great Falls
and the Falls themselves
a National Landmark

Spruce and Maple Sts. —
a whole section of the city named after trees!

Ah, to name this day after William Carlos Williams!
To honor Allen Ginsberg!
How Time heals.
How poems are balm for a city's wounds.
How poems deal with chicken pox
and mumps and broken bones.

A french-fry american cheese
coca-cola lunch in diner.

Absolute awesome tour of Great Falls
with Eugene Brooks, Bob Rosenthal,
Allen Ginsberg, Anne Waldman,
and Edith Ginsberg.

Supper at Edith's.

My candystore in Bayonne
with Allen and Tommy Wanko,
sampling giant chocolate eggcream,
milky way.
Looking at pictures
writing down mentally a Bayonne poem.

For Aunt Alta on Her Death

Eruv Pesach
4/13/76

    Son Jack broken up when confronted with words
of Aunt Alta's sudden death, shocked and saddened,

sobbed and moaned and clutched his sister Elaine,
and began his wrestling with Death-Reality, questioned
Death demanding the Why the Why of her sudden departure,
questioned the Why on Eruv Pesach, the Why, our
Family Matriarch our Seder's Guest of Honor
suddenly not with us, Why the emptiness-to-be at
our Seder table, Why the awful knowledge that he (Jack)
could not speak with her anymore, or tell her to sit,
the dishes would be taken care of.
                    So, Jack wrestled
with himself, with G-d, with Life-and-Death-questions,
knowing Aunt Alta's good deeds and Heart of Love,
wrestled with angel of Death on our livingroom floor,
rolling around in torment, seeking some solace, a logical
answer, an insight into the hard-to-accept loss.
Jack's eyes streaming tears, cheeks glistening, face
aflush, blotchy, wrestling and wrestling, attempting
acceptance but unable to accept, turning his young mind
inside out, searching in all corners as he did earlier
for Chometz just two hours before.
                    The Passover preparation
still going on in our house. Large white pot of soup
cooking and turkey just done, and Tzimmus not yet begun.
Aunt Alta had already made stuffed cabbage (one of her
specialties), and applesauce, as contribution to the
Seder. So, Jack wrestled and sought an answer this
Eruv Pesach, and he reasoned with G-d and finally
finally got an answer, and calmly said, "Miss her so
much, but she's found her freedom."

Pesach: Passover
Eruv: the day prior to
Tzimmus: a dish of flanken meat, carrots, sweet potatoes; also re-
ferred to as a chaotic state, a stew
Chometz: leavened food forbidden on Passover, such as bread

To Whitman

Painting
> sloshing words
>> to Whitman

Memorial Day
> 1976

what memories of bicentennial year
here
> in Union City?

East from Kennedy Boulevard
34th St. crossing Bergenline
near jewelry store
Jewish Center looms
men in black suits
broadbrimmed furtrimmed hats
Morning Star ceramic art center
poetry upstairs
>> in old firehouse

O Walt Whitman
O Whitman
Walt   plucky old male-nurse
what would you say today
so many Freedoms threatened
so many new wrinkles
a Manhattan judge taps
Bell Telephone
opens, microfilms America's mail,
and overcharges stamps
>> O

preRevolutionary vibes
middle-class in economic vise
taxed taxed taxed taxed
taxed and hidden taxed

subtle government follies
and not so subtle too

nitely insomniac visions
British King Georgian
and Red Scary

Spy vs Spy
System vs System
our multinational plots
make cemetery
                    of mid-east
Africa
        South America

America a vast plantation
of Bank America
Gasoline Sisters and Con Ed
controlling partners in energy networks

O the pulled-down shades of Lord North
and Roman Empire's nose for conquest
the old teaghosts still hovering
over Boston
Ahh Walt Whitman
don't we ever learn?

Ah Walt Whitman
Painter of word-rhythm on American page
Ah Whitman
your nation's State
the state of this union of states
what can we state of ourselves?
Where to flee?
The killer bee comes buzzing death
from South America
as does C.I.A. Chilean junta stench,
as newsstories and t.v.

speak between lines
about rigging and shortages
ah the cost of coffee!

What dark knowledge dooms us all
that we are unable to yet fully say?

We struggle to speak Truth
hindered by Big Control of System.

O.K. O.K. Walt Whitman
how swiftly passed the years
since 'Leaves of Grass'
one-hundred-twenty-one Illusions
since your first true American Lyrics
since your free-verse
anti-pentameter revolution
since your prophesying
since your dooming
since your celebration
since spouting your longlined

rhythmic isms of America
      if this your vast developing land
since this coming-together
      conglomerate of individual states
since this bloodied adolescent country
      of bully,
                and bullied,
                          and Bull
since N.Y. Post interpretation
      of American pleasure/sin
                                anguish
since this Blake-fabled land of change/
                          no change
since the metal fire-pellets
penetrate American Throat
and bleeds out our flesh,

since Kennedy our Captain
cut down as was your Lincoln

we can't seem to emerge
from our National Shock

where layed-off police barricade Brooklyn Bridge

where Manhattan's garbage piles up on sidewalk

where closets fill with guns
and backyard with vicious dog

Walt Whitman i see you in dream
you look strangely like latterday William Everson

i hear you in New Jersey
in birdcall near
                    above the Hudson
i hear your man-to-man 'Leaves of Grass'
rustle in love for America.

EDWARD R. SMITH

Crushed Brown

Awakened to a new clear sky
On the cutting wind across Mountain Lakes
Through crooked Route 202 glowing

Hues of yellow golden leaves
Fall for the season
Into the Ramapo River

The Weather

To grab a gut is hard
In time I
Never say that
Words are as they are
Sights as in waterfalls
That get over,
Go move
As do the goldfinches of the Pine Barrens.

Old lands, harboring pirates
Rock in the hour
As do the old men who sit alone as
I, myself do or sometimes do
As the other me
Weather does not enter this picture nor
Betty, nor old friends.

Asbury Park

Girls hug their boyfriends
with concert tickets in denim jackets.

They walk past black Atlantic,
breathing the seaweed, kelp.

Retired now, machinists kiss their
wives on the boardwalk, as the

loud music covers them. The
video arcade blast quarters

into unknown galaxies.
No one fantasizes here.

"the morning cracks to peeling . . ."

the morning cracks to peeling
paint off Bayonne's oil refinery

the black Pulaski Skyway
built by immigrant labor

against an orange line of
buildings that don't hear

the cries of children
chasing a rubber ball

I Am That Hero

I am a screeching star falling into the third dimension
I am that "poor moth boy in the moon"
I am the outlaw of Sierra Madre
I am that hero

Jersey boy with a milky face, quicker, cleaner & mean
I am nice
I am that poem of yours that smile
I am Allwood Road shuffling along

I am King Kong turning 50
I am benzine polluting Elizabeth, New Jersey's lungs
I am Voltaire's scarlet briefcase containing snow air
I was the tension of the Long Island Expressway. I am yours.

Elizabeth Anne Socolow

Driving to Work in New Jersey

i. This is the state where Lindberg flew solo
where Anne Morrow learned to live alone.
Their son was taken and these are the very woods,
they say, the kidnapper escaped to.
The roads in these hills tell stories.

This is the Garden State, green, after all.
Sod farms, chicken coops, houses full
of eggs, white barns and silos. I keep
off the interstates and highways, the exhaust
of trucks and smokestacks I thought

were all of New Jersey growing up.
It can take forever to come home
on a road this winding, the cars slow,
the air quiet. I let the tape move, recording
this solitude. Played back, it holds

their quietness of the landscape, the way
the hills roll and the colts nurse from
their mothers. This summer's day, the sheep
graze, and the cows, as always, look up
over the fence. I am recording my thoughts

on the way to work. I must cut my nails.
They will make commas and quotation marks
on the pine boards of the old farmhouse

I live in. My hands will be gentler
on the keys tomorrow. Looking up through

the trees, the layers of leaves are so thick,
the branches so intricate, I see these
could be nerve cells reaching out to the air.
Everything is a green feeler. Except the tigerlilies,
out in full force in late June.

They stick their necks into the sun, into
the roads. The cars avoid their edges
and they live. I am searching for roads
where, lucky days, I see no dead animals.
Here, people move quietly enough to respond

to a kitten strayed out from the barn.
Even the clumsy hedgehogs live and die
discreetly, not by collision. I am looking
for houses newly painted, enough money
to tend them with care. Such places

there are swings. Children reach for the sky.
the small shudder of the seat means
they have just gone inside and will come out
again after a glass of lemonade. This could be
a board game, the sudden openings from dark
into fields, a clearing where the Delaware
cuts through. A bird dips into the grill
of my car. I feel the glancing impact
in my throat. Will it live? I can protect
nothing that moves blind. My heart races
long after I see feathers cohering, moving
off in plain flight. Dutchtown, Frenchtown,
Belle Mead: the names tell the story.
Conifers press through the leaves that will fall.
Mailboxes, their tongues in the air, stay with me,

red flag up, down, messages received, and given.
The double yellow line winds like perfling

on a violin, the scrolls of our lifestuff
coded: *this way, this way, this is how to go.*
For company: announcements: Evening News.

Trentonian. Arrows on yellow signs define
the shape of these old roads, named for
local families. McMullen, Ferrara, Davis,
Cullen, Swartz, Smith. I have never been
to Wileyville or Wertsville. Between farms

new buildings, treeless as any new suburb
painted msuhroom pastels. I will cross
a creek and another. The signs will say
ONE LANE BRIDGE again and again. The car
shakes, the bridge answers, but on the road

the wheels, quicker than horses as they travel,
make their own music, grabbing the uneven surface.
Weight limit ten tons, weight limit four tons,
Weidel Realty, Stop Ahead, For Sale. The mimosa
hangs over my head. This shell of metal

moves through the tunnel of trees, through
the waving corn, the stand of phone poles
carrying their curves of messages. A red bird,
above the trees, punctuates the sky with blood.
I know why red makes me stop. Buff between

green fields, the dry, old growth of last year's
crops. Blue flowers whose names I don't know
hold pieces of the sky. Burnt Hill Road,
Hollow Road. Churches everywhere. And painted
birds, horses, flowers, rainbows on mailboxes.

Railroad RXR the sign has a big X, the sign
for wrong flanked by the sign for Right.
Right Right, I always thought as a child, stay with me.
Here it is again. Right. Right. There is

nothing wrong on a day this fresh. And
bow how passing a black-roofed white barn with
a curve this ample, there can be any wars
anywhere in a field this green, people

nowhere to be seen, I can't imagine at
the moment. The road curves like the curve
of that barn, ample, guiding me toward
the rooftop. Honeysuckle tumbles over unseen
fences making walls of green I haven't noticed

since last summer. Must go slow. One Lane
Bridge, ten miles an hour, High Fields.
Bus Stop in the middle of this thick wood,
the light of the bright morning almost shut out.
There have been three terrorist attacks

ii.   in airports this week. Zion Road intersects
Lindbergh Road. Was it here that they lived,
here the baby was stolen from, on the way,
the sign says, to Jerusalem? A joke?

Growing up, it mattered most to me that
she was a poet alone because he flew alone.
I saw how she did another kind of bivouacking
solo. It mattered next that their child
was stolen, and only incidentally where from

or where the famous flight took place.
It could have been westwards across
the continents, though there is something
about a fall into water, gentler, and more
complete—the disappearance. Once at a lake

formed by a quarry, my friend dove into
the blackness and swam a half mile to the other
side. There was no rope and I did not take
her dare, though then, alone on the near shore,
how he flew, in darkness over the Atlantic.

Rachel Carson was my hero and my father said:
"She never married." I knew she was married
to the land, trying to save it, knew she was
married to the sea she rode and wrote of, inward,
against smothering. In another century

she might have found a companionable husband.
And I knew it was better for the Lindberghs
that they were married. Surely it is always
kinder to have someone to think of, in particular,
as you fly solo in the wilderness. Huge rocks
are hitting the belly of my car on this road
that is being newly graded. I am moving slower
and slower. I must care for the belly of my car.
I am no tractor. And if there were people
with me here, I might break into song now,

caught behind this rolling truck. It must
have a fine name with its large, heavy cylinder
it pushes like an ant a crumb. I keep thinking.
I think I have just turned the wrong way.
In fact, I'm sure. I need to turn back.

An old man pulls by the side of the road
in a pick-up, green, and he is frowning because
he can't turn till I've gone by. He means
to get it right, leisurely and accurate.
I love these men who work farms and know

the ways of women, chickens, things that grow.
I love the way they talk. And even though
I'm traveling wrong now, it is so calm and pretty,
it doesn't matter. I must go back. But there
is a red barn just ahead, and I am coming

to a crossroad. They all lead to 202 and 31.
They all take me where I am going. There is
no wrong turn, just better ways, and less good,

Elizabeth Anne Socolow 197

to turn in. Knives, scissors, clippers, blades.
they are sharpened here expertly. There is

a right way to do it, and a particular place
to sink steel. Al's Gun Repair is just across
the street. I am in Reaville. I will have to
go through other armed villages before I ever
get to Baptisttown and Frenchtown.

Pleasant Bridge Memorial park, the sign says.
It stands across from the old cemetery in Amwell.
And that is what this ride is, a pleasant bridge
from sleep to working, and back. I cross over
from moment to moment. I cross over synapse

and creek. The street lamps here reach
into the street like a bridge stopped short.
Roiling water below. And there has been a life
stopped short in this season, I always remember,
a woman snatched too soon, like a kidnapped child.

This air bring her mother's laughter, laughter of her
own eyes digging the garden of the man she loved,
yellow irises with brown flecks like swimming carp
in a pond. Everyone born, every child that leaves
before the time is right is a sacrifice. Season's

Greetings. That's what a day like this says.
On these back roads where I pretend there is
little death, it's only that I am trying
not to notice. And keep remembering the truth is:
we are not all alive.

The Tack You Take

This afternoon, since seeing the stopped tan car,
I keep coming to that place on a lake where the texture of the
    water
goes from black to gray, smooth to tweed. I know it is only a
    matter of light
moving differently across and in and out the little waves
the wind has stirred.

In this boat, in this hour, I see
the difference between smooth black and rough gray
is a matter of crossing borders, stitches fastening a hem.
The light itself is thread, waves, or cascades of small bits
    of matter
coming to the water.

This is the way the boat tacks in and out the coarse salt and dark
    eye of the lake,
the way a mood enters an ordinary afternoon
and calls for ropes, sails,
muscle straining against the wind.

At noon, I saw an open door of a police car, lights flashing and
    a blue striped leg
sticking out the second open door, the stopped tan car.
From a distance I thought *speeding*, I thought *ticket* until I saw
    no driver,
the heaving of what may have been a rescue,
the officer's breath forced down the throat of someone dead.
I wanted to stop and did not. How could I help a policeman?

This is the way the wind moves across a still place
where we could drown for the lifelessness, the way half our
    afternoons
summon us to action.

To a Friend in Fear

I know from those nights alone on the river.
Even with the other campers near,
the bear looms larger than he is.
My flashlight is my proof against disaster,
sure as a lonely lighthouse, less prominent,
small torch. When you say there has been
bleeding, the doctor has ordered tests, I am shocked
and fearful for hours without speaking. I imagine
you gone, my life dull as the eyes of a cat left alone in a house,
the body giving in to sleep.

Lying

A lie is a kind of gap
like an open door
through which anything
can enter as trouble, new shoes
blistering the feet, lavender
shaving soap calling up
memories of a lost time.
It would be a lie to say
I've never let that mischief govern
what I've spoken or that trouble is not
delayed by the telling of what isn't altogether
true. But I want those I know best,
love most to level, as we say,
speak plain as a smooth road,
easy to walk in the sun.

Bamboo Indoors at the Corporate Center

Bamboo, I mean a whole grove of green stalks
slender as teenager girls, and lithe and light
under the glass canopy of many peaks
like the crystal palace or the great
glass railway stations of the late nineteenth
century, I say bamboo, as if this were the tropics.
It grows in a vaulted space of air so still
and cool despite the 90 degree heat outside
not one leaf lifts, or bends.

The notched trunks measure growth and seasons like a ruler,
no numbers marked in a jungle of such vast silence
no birds sing, no tigers stalk the leaves.
Here there is no waste. Even the columns are smooth.
And I ache for the scallop fluting, wanting the tides
that change and call out the dips and hills of shells
and breath. O this is a place of power—liquids, jellies,

creams here are made, marketed from this calm
ease, this security of no unwanted life, these thin
trees chosen to live like girls not yet women, not
yet, or ever to be filled with pandas and the stones
below never noised by hunger, never graced by musk,
or the weight of feet exploring, moving in the air,
attending the unrestrained sky,
the hushed balance of 613 species of beetle alone
clustered in harmony on the topmost branches of a true
forest where it rains.

MADELINE TIGER

The Gull

the huge grey gull
over the Jersey Turnpike
steely as Amtrak

crosses long above this
congestion, soars
toward the seashore

his wings waving slowly

his beak points beyond
our dull metal,
grey as we've made him

he's traversing our lines
of bright cars, hot motors
rushed and stalled
        in their own fumes

far up he glides, he is
pointing to shining water,

to the waves that glisten—
ripples, breakers
with fierce bursting crests—

and when he squawks out there,

his cry leaves a whiteness
in the mind of the driver

The Belleville Girl

In Belleville, New Jersey it's spring. The shops
open onto the small bustle of streets full of
everyone's business. I've been delivering
lectures on educating restless adolescents in view of
the bridges and smokestacks of Kearny—
with a smoggy New York City skyline in the distance.
My eye has been wandering quite widely over this
cluttered landscape, my native land! it's so close
and so disconnected; my tongue is loose. I drive on
through the spring city, eclectic.
Belleville: A chubby little girl, about twelve or
thirteen, with budding breasts and a fat tummy—
like the tummies I remember from summer camp when
we knew the love of marshmallows and uncontrollable
giggles, the distaste for tennis, the secret pride of
sanitary napkins, the uneasy respect for our dour
counselors—that momentarily acceptable fat—
she has squeezed into tight black tights (they may
be pants) pulled around her belly and down almost
to her ankles above which wrapping she's wearing
a strapless pink tank top all shirred and wrinkling over
her plumpness and her little breasts (Imagination plays
optimistically with baby fat). Her hair is all wispy
and she's wearing a slanted half-smile but with a de-
termined eye as if she had in mind what to buy, at ex-
actly which shop and for how much and at the same time
how to walk straight click click with a slight lilt (it
could be a sway or a wiggle) to her chunky backside,
which I suspect she thinks is already an ass, with hips
(or maybe she's recently been raped by her father or
uncle or brother and is managing pretty well, considering,
to overcome that) keeping time to some tune she's pleased
pink to know by heart, and dreaming of a slim boy who
might be, or might soon be, the Boyfriend, from tenth
grade, with a little moustache; or so she pretends,

nonchalant as her older sister whose pants she's
wearing, whose top she's just found and fit into with
more excitement than all the mall-bent blue-nailed hair-
teased buxom girls gathered on the front stoops
of spring in Belleville & Bloomfield & (yes, even) Glen
Ridge & Montclair, America, circa these Eighties, can feel
or can remember from their lost youths.

While We Were Thinking of
Ginkgo Leaves

the box shook with world news
the stock market collapsed
wild man Brodsky won the Nobel Prize
"and yet and yet and yet"
the news: My sister Babs called
in a great voice of money
from California and the children
traveled—to Paris, to Vienna,
to Copenhagen, across the wide
and shining sea of thee oh freedom
and air; the birds were everywhere:
great geese honking across Brookdale Pond
and the mallards in pairs preening
their green luminescent necks
all shiny in the cold noon glare
Sunday the sun came slanting
down and held the universe over
the green red gold blue town

Autumn Poem

October
in California
azaleas larger
than azaleas
open
bougainvillea flourish with
profusions of crimson hibiscus,
and fuchsia

a heavy lemon tree
hangs fruit over
the pool
while dead leaves
drop steadily
from some   where
flies circle / buzz
in my hair

I'm homesick for
the bleak autumn East
the *in doors*
the closing & locking &
comfort of my corner
my desk my lamp my chair
the tiny crabapple fruit
and the crow
in the blue spruce
the yellow, red, gold that explodes   and
slowly in one long week after harvest
disappears into shapeless heaps of dark
I'm homesick for the inescapable
damp mulching
into earth and *the earth* there
and the sharp touch
of the air

Name and Place

for Howard Tiger, Newark, 1976

My father tells me he believed
men would not be different from each other,
Jew from Gentile, by the time he was old;
my father climbed all over greening Abe Lincoln
sitting there big and bronze in front of the fearful
courthouse among pigeons and tenement fires.
My father said he looked up to the hills,
he was a happy boy with no money, his violin,
his strudel kitchen, his prank strings
October nights on Belmont Avenue, his father
chuckling home with pockets and
little white paperbags of sweetcakes Saturdays.
My father said a kitchen always rang tomato soup,
families are loyal even when Tiger gambled,
left them stitch poor and Elsie in the attic
fixing patterns, the others near spinsters.
My father told me he was American he worked
hard he made it land of opportunity up hill
Hallowe'en bonfires long since and even though
it was hard to find the house on Fairmont Avenue,
still we knew the name "Tiger" was in the lintel,
the name that old tailor took landing in
this place and before he went gambling,
the name he left them, the lost name,
the name of no sons and no grandsons

If you have a land
and you know the color of the soil
wet in your hands and it has been
your father's land and his father's
before him through the thick dis-
comfort of crude shoes tromping
marking the middle of some great

continent, if it had been so
for generations, then
even if it was not given
by feudal apportionment,
even if your family's name
was only written on pain
and the government doesn't know
how they came, how long tolerated,
how tithed, even if it had not been
their land except by knowledge and
certain colors early in the morning
out past the fields, certain
sweetness of straw, spring wine
sipped in a young girl's mouth or
a sense of dig, and sleep
past seasons, past the deaths
of women in childbirth; if
you have even a crumb of such a story,
of such a land, then
it doesn't matter if you are not a man
to give a name
to your father's name
to do his labor
under this name
in the new city
to engrave this name
on the lintel of houses
to write this name
in a black Bible
to pronounce this name
in a new language
to grow old in its shade
to recognize your father
to nominate him
when you are the elder
in this name;
to present him with sons.

If there is a land
you walked in together
or a stand of blue spruce and gnarled pine
you watched together
and he told you about the samplings,
your name matters less: you can be
a daughter who does not exist
for the sake of a name.

But we have come
washed out of history,
escaped or banished, the cause indifferent,
our parts dispersed
long before we knew a homeland
long after we knew a homeland
furrowed with familiar trees,
with no connection to our fathers' steps
on earth unanchored to streets and sidewalks.
We've come with only the glittering hopes:
the wild new alphabet
in a girl's notebook,
the long brown hair of buxom peasants
with strong arms and brave tongues,
the ancient love-moon behind shops
and a cold sun to cut out the days,
to make the cement seem to shine
gold and silver. Johanna Rose dreamed,
cooking and saving, giving birth,
and starting ocean stories
hundreds of times over, to carve
at last the new name over the door
of a house in Newark, to mark our place,
to pray for sons. We have only
this amazing passage.

I have no roots in soil or language,
I have no place to dig for my caul,

only skyline and pavement of a steel city
to look back on and know
for the name's sake
to know my father
whose name is wasting,
to give him a land,
to re-create.

ROD TULLOSS

By the canal near Griggstown

from a long way across the flats and their dried grasses
           (seeing the way the land lies, the
           way grass lies in the flood plain—
           pointing
           the last current's course),
across all this gray / white / beige and
under the gray / white / beige light of winter sky slit with blue,
under all this,
the dust rising behind my son's feet like smoke—
as if their small flames escape
spotting brushfires through the field.
I will stand in this tall hollow trunk about the woodchuck
   hole and
show myself when called.
I'm cold.
I love them.
That's all.

*xii.*7.75

Drifts

Here on the field's edge,
uncut weeds are the slim ghosts of dancers.

The snow reminds this one of great Spanish coiffures:
and wind, of her heels' sharp clacking.

And one dreams without desire
of pale fishes subtly curling at dusk.

Even though the wind is steady,
it is all a stillness.

The drifts
move onto small country roads.

i.2.78
Quaker Bridge Mall
for Mary

Seed

Blown red sumac stretches east.
In the windswept stretch before our garden,
seed tops from a tall wild grass tumble—
fine-threaded ghost cocoons.
In your illness, it is a pleasure to see
things without strength or mass
filling their places untouched
by a sense of purpose.

x.29.83
Cape May
for Mary

"the path back . . ."

the path back
from the post off-
                    ice, black-
birds flushed from cherry trees.
The ragged flights, the
flock, the rain, the
trees, in-
terstices.

vii.30.77
Roosevelt
for David Herrstrom

Error

The crow again.
Every winter I see him, early
on my way to work,
rowing crystal air at zero
with tiny slow turns
at the tips of his wings,
his eye intent
no matter where he glances.
Every year I want this of him:
the smallest bit
of the least particle of God—
to be known once
like a stone or pain.

In the Midst of Reading Wang Wei

The new pipe darkens slowly.
The afternoon brightens.
Every month since I've known you
I become more happy.
When people greet me,
I tell them *how I am*.
Isn't it odd they keep asking?

xi.1–6.77
Chicago/Roosevelt
for Mary

LOIS VAN HOUTEN

Sixes & Sevens

Here's my dream, now
my front porch in dream
scope . . .

the seven steps to the stoop
where I sit with Evie & Phillip
& Joe
pebble tucked in fist.

Here's the hammock where I
played doctor with Ruth Ann
and read Seven Keys to Baldpate.

Seven plants on their little
tables . . . a profusion of
leaves.
(I never learned where they
came from.)

Here's the window where I
melted my finger against the
wind:
the sand still lays on the sill:
the grass rug that no one swept
the table with the wicker-bodied
lamp.

Here I am, woke up at sixty
squint-eyed as a bat. A
cold wind curling my face has
done me in.

Streets I Know

streets I know
where the houses grow
like mushrooms under their dotty roofs
streets of pain
fences / loose from their pickets
raggedy-ann dolls, lying about
unsocketed.
these streets where people and cats
prowl about scruffily
from nine to nine:
even on good days
a bitter smell of crushed insects
hangs about the woodwork;
even on mild days
there are too many red-eyed grandmothers
too much soot from the furnaces . . .

and in the house of nineteen persons
there are nineteen strangers
all, the same eyes and mouth . . . on these streets
where the home for unwed mothers
decays behind a spike-toothed wall
and a wild wisteria
plaits the eyes of the damned
on these streets
there are no falcons at the wrist
straining for flight
but only sparrows who peck

absently at the droppings
under the pedlar's
cart.

Rain / Night Song

tonight we have mandarin
soup in a chinese aviary

outside's wet as a leather glove
rain spokes the trees   chinese
lanterns float the streets

the room's sealed off . the
Szechuan waiter   leans in the
slant of his eyes

listen   the nightingales sing
their enameled songs   their
eyes are saffroned gold

a white man balances a black
woman on a black child :
they love each other   bow
to them

tomorrow , the dogs will pick
frog legs   again   from the
garbage cans .

Whinny for My Quick

The old lights are winking , again
On Clay St. , Market , Madison and Cantrell
And over Vince's , Victor's and Vi's
Barber shop , and Pete's.
Pickles and peanuts to the cigar-store
Indian , Moe Mokum . . . . . and voices
Burped like smoke from a genie-jar
Gently jostle me.

For I have played touch-me , touch-me ,
Too many times among the tombstones:
And therefore, now ,am one with ghosts.
And like the goose-chased sunset
Unrolling red and gold over a fallen
Day, I look back, rearing like a
Stray stallion and whinny
For my quick.

THEODORE WEISS

'Yes, But . . .'

for WCW again

There he was—having spent
the night with us, the first
time away from home alone,

terribly frail for another stroke,
his dreams still shaking him—
his fame steadily leaping ahead,

and he complaining to me,
struggling just to be somebody,
expecting me to comfort him!

Manfully, if with a bitter sense
of injustice, I did my best:
'Why, Bill, you've left a good
green swath of writing behind you.'

And he, in a low voice,
most mournfully, 'Yes, but
is it poetry?'
        That years ago.
Only now I begin to understand
the doubts necessary to one
always open, always desperate
(his work's honesty, spontaneity—
work nothing, life—depended
on it),

one too so given
over to the moment, so lover-
faithfully serving it,
he could remember or believe
in little else,
                    (Some months
later Frost would visit,
older, sturdy as an ancient oak,
unlike Williams, who could not read
to the end of a verse,
                    intoning
his poems well over an hour
with tremendous relish, then
standing on his solid stumps
another hour batting it out
with students,
                    no doubts shaking
him and few new leaves breaking
out of him.)
                    And only now,
the years, the doubts accumulating,
can I be grateful to Bill
for his uncertainty,
                    can I lean
on it, lean more than on all
his accomplishments, those greeny
asphodel triumphs.

The Good Grey Poet

Look to your words, old man,
for the original intelligence, the wisdom
buried in them. Know however that it
surfaces when it will. Perfect comrades

words have been, constant like few others
in your loneliness. But they too have a life
and a time of their own. Responding to
the slow, essential music of their natures,
they must go their ways as you go yours.

After so many throes, so many convulsions,
not only a war that threatened to tear
your world to pieces, the world you had
most ambitiously dreamed, all the pieces
of bodies you had seen stacked under a tree,
the maggots working overtime, but deaths
accumulating of those dearest to you,
politics, conviviality, love, the rest
at last exhausted, do you not hear hints
from the vantage point of what you've become?

Your ideal, you wrote a healthy time ago
to guide yourself, was Merlin: "strong
& wise & beautiful at 100 years old."
Strong & wise since "his emotions &c are
complete in himself. . . . He grows, blooms,
like some perfect tree or flower, in Nature,
whether viewed by admiring eyes or in
some wild or wood entirely unknown."

For your liver fattening, the cyst ripening
in your adrenal, the left lung collapsed,
the right perhaps an eighth suitable
for breathing, a big stone rattled round
in your gallbladder (righter than you knew,
you were—and even at the time you wrote,
rock-bottom feelings under you, your poems—
truly incorporating gneiss!), the ball
of string tangled in the gut like a clue
to knit up all contrarieties, you must be
more and more yourself.
                              Often, leaning

against a ferry rail, the sea your company,
your words beat out a rhythm so continuous
inside your body that you hardly noticed it,
content to let its current carry you along,
wherever it took you your place.
                                    Now
you, who thought—sufficient stores laid in—
that your awareness had already pierced
the distant future, view these phrases
and that rhythm, still pursuing their course,
as any stranger might.
                              Your doubt does not
surprise. Who can miss the unexpected things
emerged to startle you, even waking shame
and fear?
              But then you surely realize
how lucky you are, not only to have them,
these words, striking out on their own,
bearded with faces you scarcely recognize,
refusing to bend to your wishes or regrets,
refusing to acknowledge you in any way,
but to be able to use them—most because
they refuse—to measure that essential music
as it, and at its own sweet pace, moves on
to find the latest version of the truth
in the changes it is making.
                                    Beyond that,
your words work, and work for you, by what
they do to others, bringing you—this
from far-off continents—reports of pleasure,
love, the tender might your poems go on
gathering as they inspire it.
                                    And those,
the first breezy verses informing the winds,
your words in all their youthful innocence,
become so different, yet so much themselves,
like fruits more and more are bearing, bearing
out their father tree.

Notes on Contributors

AMIRI BARAKA (formerly Leroi Jones) has been a major force in American letters since the early sixties. Born in Newark in 1934, he returned to that city in 1966 (after living in Manhattan for a decade) and has lived there since. A contemporary Renaissance man, he has written masterful plays, novels, short stories, essays, and musical criticism in addition to his highly influential poetry. His *Selected Poems* (1979) is a well-chosen, comprehensive collection. He is a poet in the tradition of Pablo Neruda and Aime Cesaire, seeing no dichotomy in being a writer and a political activist. A professor of African-American Studies at SUNY/Stony Brook, he spent the 1988–89 academic year as a visiting professor at Rutgers/New Brunswick. "Money" and "ALLIFESTO" are published here for the first time.

KENNETH BURKE is perhaps best known in this country as a brilliant and singular philosopher-critic whose writings have had enormous influence on The New Criticism, Deconstructionism and Marxist literary theory. Volumes such as *Counter-Statement* (1931) and *A Grammar of Motives* (1945) remain essential works of literary criticism. Few of his admirers, however, are aware of his fine poetry, which was collected in a volume by University of California Press in 1968. Born in 1897, he has lived in the Sussex County community of Andover since the mid-twenties. Still active, he continues to lecture and teach around the country, while continuing his work as both a scholar and a poet. His most recent book was a volume of correspondence with Malcolm Cowley. He was awarded the National Medal for Literature in 1981.

JOSEPH CERAVOLO, whose work was praised by both Kenneth Rexroth and John Ashbery, died while this volume was in preparation. A resident of Bloomfield, Ceravolo wrote his poetry while maintaining a career as a civil engineer. His first book, *Spring in This World of Poor Mutts*, was published by Columbia University Press and was winner of the first Frank O'Hara Award for Poetry. His most recent volume was *Millennium Dust* (1982). "Winter," "Still Life," and "Rifle Shot" are from the manuscript *Mad Angel (Poems 1984–1988)*.

CHERYL CLARKE is the author of *Narratives: Poems in the Tradition of Black Women* (1983) and *Living as a Lesbian* (1986). A member of the feminist *Conditions* magazine collective since 1981, her poems, stories, and essays have been published in numerous anthologies and magazines. She works and lives in Jersey City.

DINA COE worked as flight attendant for an international airline for twenty years before devoting her full time to writing. She has won two grants for poetry from the New Jersey State Council on The Arts (NJSCA), as well as an Academy of American Poets Prize.

TOI DERRICOTTE is the author of *the Empress of The Death House* (1979), *Natural Birth* (1983) and *Captivity* (1989). Her worked has been praised by both Audre Lorde and Adrienne Rich and she recently received a special master poet grant from the NJSCA. A long-time resident of Essex Fells, she recently has been teaching creative writing at Old Dominion College in Virginia.

STEPHEN DUNN is a professor of creative writing at Stockton State College. He has published five volumes of poetry, the most recent being *Local Time* (1984) and *Between Angels* (1989). He has been an NEA Fellow in addition to holding Fellowships from the NJSCA and the Breadloaf Workshop. He lives in Port Republic.

SEAN T. FARRAGHER was born in Edgewater, a small industrial town below the Palisades and hard against the Hudson. His *Narrative of the New Netherlands* (1977) reflects a lifelong interest in the history of the Hudson River. After a hiatus from the poetry scene, he has become active once again and was the subject of a recent profile in *Gold Coast* magazine. He lives in Palisades Park.

ALLEN GINSBERG is America's most famous living poet. His *Howl* (1956) changed the course of English-language poetry, opening the door to a period of innovation and experimentation that has yet to run its course. Born and raised in Paterson, his father was the respected lyric poet Louis Ginsberg. Approaching William Carlos Williams on the pretense of interviewing him, Ginsberg impressed

Williams enough for the doctor to write introductions to the younger poet's first two volumes of poetry. His *Collected Poems* (1984) is essential reading to any serious student of contemporary poetry. *White Shroud* (1986) is his most recent volume, with volumes of his letters and essays forthcoming. He is currently teaching poetry at Brooklyn College.

MAX GREENBERG began writing poetry at age sixty, after many years as a social worker/administrator in New York and New Jersey. He was a NJSCA Fellow in 1981 and 1984. His *Country of The Old* was published in 1982. He is currently conducting poetry workshops with the elderly in Riverdale and upper Manhattan. He lives in Passaic.

ALFRED STARR HAMILTON has been referred to by poet Larry Fagin as the "Joseph Cornell of American poetry." Except for a few years in the Army during World War II, he has lived all his life in Montclair as a semi-recluse, where he was fined (in true Thoreau fashion) for refusing to go indoors during a civil defense drill in 1961. His *Poems of Alfred Starr Hamilton* (1970), published by Jonathan Williams's Jargon Society press, has become something of a cult item, fetching high prices by rare book collectors. A more recent book, *The Big Parade*, was published in 1982.

JIM HANDLIN has had poetry published in *Poetry*, *Prairie Schooner*, *Pequod*, and numerous others. A two-time NJSCA Fellow, he also was awarded the New School's Dylan Thomas Prize in 1979. He lives in Plainfield and is headmaster of the upper school of the Pingry School in Martinsville.

PENNY HARTER is the author of eight volumes of poetry, including *White Flowers in The Snow*, *Lovepoems* and *The Price of Admission*. A three-time NJSCA Fellow, she worked for ten years in the state's Poetry in the Schools program (PITS). In 1987, she won the Mary Carolyn Davies Memorial Award from the Poetry Society of America. She lives in Scotch Plains.

WILLIAM J. HIGGINSON moved to Paterson in 1969, inspired by reading William Carlos Williams's *Paterson*. His decade in the Silk City was documented in *Paterson Pieces: Poems 1969–1979*. A translator of Japanese poetry, he is the author of *The Haiku Handbook: How to Write, Share & Teach Haiku* (1985). His latest collection is *Healing & Other Poems* (1986). He lives in Scotch Plains.

MARK HILLRINGHOUSE, the former poetry director for the William Carlos Williams Center for the Arts in Rutherford, has worked as an editor for the *New York Arts Journal* and *American Book Review*. He is currently an administrator and creative writing instructor at Passaic County Community College. His poetry, articles and interviews have appeared in *Sequoia, The Little Magazine, American Poetry, Mag City,* and others. A two-time NJSCA Fellow, he lives in East Orange.

ELIOT KATZ is the author of *Thieves at Work* (1988). A graduate of Rutgers University, he is a proofreader/printer as well as a political activist. The organizer of uncountable readings in New York and New Jersey, he is also a co-founder of *Long Shot* magazine. He lives in New Brunswick.

DAVID KELLER says that he "likes to think of himself as educated in the orchestra pits and theatres of the Boston area, despite holding degrees from Harvard and the University of Wisconsin." A member of the US 1 Poet's Cooperative, his books include *A New Room* (1987) and *Land That Wasn't Ours* (1989). He lives in Roosevelt.

BRIGIT PEGEEN KELLY's first book of poems, *To The Place of Trumpets* was selected by James Merrill to be the winning volume of the Yale Series of Younger Poets. Among her many awards are NEA and NJSCA Fellowships and *The Nation's* 1986 Discovery Award. She lives in Branchville.

AUGUST KLEINZAHLER is the author of five volumes of poetry, the most recent being *Earthquake Weather* (1989). One of his poems was seen by millions of commuters on the mass transit systems of New York City, Chicago, Washington D.C., and Los Angeles when it appeared as a bus placard in *Streetfare Journal: The Magazine of the Rider*. The winner of two NJSCA Fellowships and a General Electric Younger Writer Award, he was writer-in-residence at the University of California at Berkeley in 1988. He lives in Fort Lee.

JOEL LEWIS has lived most of his life in Hudson County, never too far from the shadows cast by the massive and solonic Manhattan skyline. His books include *Three Works* (1983) and *Entropia* (1986). His poetry, critical essays and reviews have appeared in *Sulfur*, *Caliban*, *American Book Review*, and others. An NJSCA Fellow in 1983, he currently hangs his beret in Hoboken.

GERALDINE C. LITTLE is the author of *A Well-Tuned Harp* (1988) and *Heloise and Abelard: The Drama in Verse* (1989). Born in Ireland, she is vice-president of The Poetry Society of America (PSA) and has won awards from the PSA, PEN, and the NJSCA. She is also a musician, performing with the Choral Arts Society of Philadelphia. She lives in Mount Holly.

DOUGHTRY "DOC" LONG is the author of *Song for Nia, Black Love Black Hope*, and *Poetry*. A former Peace Corp volunteer in Sierra Leone, he has taught English and Creative Writing in both the New York City and Trenton school systems. He was a NJSCA Fellow in 1983.

PABLO MEDINA is an assistant professor of English and Spanish at Mercer County Community College who has conducted poetry workshops in settings ranging from the New Jersey Teen Arts Festival to Rahway State Prison. His *Pork Rind and Cuban Songs* appeared in 1975. A two-time NJSCA Fellow, he lives in Pennington.

JOYCE CAROL OATES is the author of twenty-one novels and numerous volumes of short stories and critical essays. Her stature as a literary critic and one of America's premiere writers of fiction has overshadowed an active and productive career as a poet. Since 1969 she has published five volumes of poetry, including the *Invisible Woman* (1982), a collection of selected poems. She lives in Princeton.

ALICIA OSTRIKER enjoys distinguished careers as a William Blake scholar, a feminist theorist, and a poet. Many of us have her magisterial edition of *William Blake, The Complete Poems* in our libraries, while two volumes of her criticism, *Writing Like A Woman* and *Stealing The Language*, have helped define the feminist literary project. Her poetry reflects the consistency of vision and craft of her scholarly and critical work and includes the volumes *Songs* (1969), *A Woman Under The Surface* (1982), *The Imaginary Lover* (1986), and *Green Age* (1989). She is a professor of English at Rutgers University, New Brunswick, and lives in Princeton.

JAMES RUGGIA was declared by no less an authority than Allen Ginsberg to be "the verse poet of tender complexities and driving compulsions." He is the author of *Crossing the Border* (1985) and a forthcoming volume of selected poems. In addition, he has written numerous travel pieces, mostly based on extended residences in Turkey and Central America. He was project director for the Writers-in-the-Schools program in the Hoboken school system, teaching over ninety workshops and editing two anthologies of children's art and writings. A resident of Hoboken since before its gentrification, he is currently at work on a novel.

DAVID SHAPIRO published his first book poetry, *January* (1965), when he was eighteen years old and has published five volumes since, the most recent being *House (Blown Apart)* (1988). He wrote the first book-length study of the poetry of John Ashbery and was co-editor of the highly influential *An Anthology of New York Poets* (1970). An NEA Fellow and recipient of the 1977 Morton Dauwen Zabel Award from the American Academy and Institute of Arts and Letters, he has written widely on contemporary art, including a monograph on Jasper Johns. Currently, he is associate professor of Art History at William Paterson College of New Jersey.

HERSCHEL SILVERMAN is the author of *Krishna Poems* (1969), *Nite Train* (1973), and *Elegies* (1979), among many volumes. A 1980 NJSCA Fellow, he was the subject of a video-documentary directed by J. J. Murphy. In 1989 *Scrap Paper Review* devoted their first chapbook to Silverman's poetry. He was the owner-operator of a candy store, Hersh's Beehive, for over forty years in Bayonne, becoming something of a local celebrity, known both for his poetry and his authentic egg creams.

EDWARD R. SMITH is the author of *Dwasline Road* (1983) and *By The Green Pool* (1985). A life-long resident of that archetypal suburb Clifton, he is currently a graduate student in the creative writing program at Rutgers/Newark. His work was anthologized in *The Temple of*

Baseball and the *Beehive Anthology*, with reviews and poems having appeared in *Action, Big Scream,* and *The Poetry Project Newsletter.*

ELIZABETH ANNE SOCOLOW's *Laughing At Gravity: Conversations With Isaac Newton* (1988) was winner of the 1987 Barnard Women Poets Award. She is a founding member of the US 1 Poet's Cooperative and currently coordinates the reading series for the Arts Council of Princeton. A two-time winner of NJSCA Fellowships, her current project is the translation of the Bulgarian poet Blaga Dimitrova, in collaboration with Ludmilla Wightman. She teaches creative writing at both Barnard and Vassar and lives in Princeton.

MADELINE TIGER is the author of *Toward Spring Bank* (1981) and *Keeping House In This Forest* (1977). Her poetry was included in *We Become New,* one of the first women's poetry anthologies, and has also been published in magazines such as *Ikon* and *The New Republic.* A three-time NJSCA Fellow, she is co-author, with Toi Derricotte, of *Creative Writing: A Manual for Teachers* (1985). She has lived in Upper Montclair since 1963.

ROD TULLOSS is the author of *December 1975* (1976) and *The Machine Shuts Down* (1982). His poetry has appeared in *Exquisite Corpse, Nimrod,* and other magazines. He is a founder of both the Berkeley Poets Co-op and the US 1 Poet's Cooperative and has twice won NJSCA Fellowships.

LOIS VAN HOUTEN is the author of six volumes of poetry, the most recent being *Coming To Terms With Geese* (1988). Many local writers have attended craft workshops that she has conducted over the last twenty years, particularly those sponsored by the Bergen Poets in Fair Lawn. She has won grants form the NJSCA, the Dodge Foundation, and Poets & Writers of New York, Inc. She lives in Fair Lawn.

THEODORE WEISS is a familiar name to any serious reader of contemporary American poetry. His *From Princeton One Autumn Afternoon: Collected Poems of Theodore Weiss* (1987) summarizes a distinguished career that includes ten books of poetry and four volumes of criticism. With his wife Renée, he edits *Quarterly Review of Literature.* A winner of numerous awards, fellowships, and grants, he recently retired as a professor of English at Princeton University.

Acknowledgments

We would like to thank the following individuals and publishers for permission to reprint material copyrighted or controlled by them:

Amiri Baraka and Sterling Lord Literistic, Inc., for "In Memory of Radio," "Cops," and "Cold Term"; copyright © 1980 by Amiri Baraka. Amiri Baraka for "Against Bourgeois Art," "A Contract," "Money," and "ALLIFESTO!"; copyright © by Amiri Baraka.

Kenneth Burke and the University of California Press for poems from *Collected Poems, 1915–1945*. (Berkeley and Los Angeles: University of California Press, 1968); copyright © 1968 by Kenneth Burke.

The Estate of Joseph Ceravolo for "The Wind Is Blowing West," from *Spring in This World of Poor Mutts* (New York: Columbia University Press, 1968; Full Court, 1978), copyright © 1968 by Joseph Ceravolo; "A Railway Stop," "Night Birds," "Meadowlands," and "Park Thoughts," from *Millennium Dust* (New York: Kulchur Press, 1982), copyright © 1982 by Joseph Ceravolo; "Rte. 3 into N.Y.," from *Ahnoi #3* (1980), copyright © 1980 by Joseph Ceravolo; "Rifle Shot," "Winter," and "Still Life," from "Mad Angels (1984–1988)" copyright © by the Estate of Joseph Ceravolo. No part of these poems may be reproduced in any means without written permission from the abovementioned Estate.

Cheryl Clarke for "Of Althea and Flaxie," from *Narratives: Poems in the Tradition of Black Women* (Latham, N.Y.: Kitchen Table Press, 1983), copyright © 1983 by Cheryl Clarke. Cheryl Clarke and Firebrand Books for "jazz poem for Morristown, N.J." and "the layoff," from *Living as a Lesbian* (Ithaca, N.Y.: Firebrand Books, 1986), copyright © 1986 by Cheryl Clarke. Cheryl Clarke for "Bulletin," from *Humid Pitch* (Ithaca, N.Y.: Firebrand Books, forthcoming), copyright © 1990 by Cheryl Clarke.

Diana Coe for "Manhattan, Now That I Don't Live There," "Garden Journal, November," and "Midsummers' Eve Day"; copyright © by Diana Coe.

Penny Harter for "A Man Beside the New Jersey Turnpike, Easter Eve," from *Footwork* (1987) copyright © 1987 by Penny Harter; "At the Mall" and "Reading the Tea Leaves"; copyright © by Penny Harter. "Mattress Fire," from *The Price of Admission* (Fanwood, N.J.: From Here Press, 1986), copyright © 1986 by Penny Harter.

William J. Higginson and Old Plate Press for "The Passaic Falls, October," "Paterson: Spring Exotic," "Spring in Paterson, I," and "Spring in Paterson, II," from *Paterson Pieces: Poems 1969–1979* (Fanwood, N.J.: Old Plate Press, 1981), copyright © 1981 by William J. Higginson. William J. Higginson and From Here Press for "Nanna's Soap," from *Death Is & Approaches to the Edge* (Fanwood, N.J.: From Here Press, 1981), copyright © 1981 by William J. Higginson.

Mark Hillringhouse for "In Paterson," "Cianci Street," "Dear Walt," and "Leaving Paterson," from *Longshot* #8 (1988), copyright © by Mark Hillringhouse.

Eliot Katz for "As I Stand Before Your Grave, Camerado," "After Ten Years, So Long New Brunswick," and "How Many More Nights?" from *Thieves at Work*, copyright © 1988 by Eliot Katz.

David Keller and Carnegie-Mellon University Press for "Stopping for Breakfast," "Going Back to the City," and "The Chinese Written Character as a Medium for Poetry," from *Land That Wasn't Ours* (Pittsburgh: Carnegie-Mellon University Press, 1989), copyright © 1989 by David Keller. David Keller and the *Quarterly Review of Literature* for "Longing" and "Crossing the States" from *A New Room* (Princeton, N.J.: Quarterly Review of Literature, 1987). David Keller for "At the Edge of the Continent"; copyright © by David Keller.

Brigit Pegeen Kelly and Yale University Press for "Doing Laundry on Sunday" and "The House on Main Street," from *To the Place of Trumpets* (New Haven: Yale University Press, 1988), copyright © 1988 by Brigit Pegeen Kelly.

August Kleinzahler and Mayer Bell Ltd. for "November in West New York," "Poetics," "Storm over Hackensack," and "Canada Geese in New Jersey," from *Storm Over Hackensack* (Mount Kisco, N.Y.: Moyer Bell Ltd., 1985) and "On the Way Home to New Jersey One Night," from *Earthquake Weather* (Mount Kisco, N.Y.: Moyer Bell Ltd., 1989); copyright © by August Kleinzahler.

Joel Lewis for "Pushing the Envelope," "Cape May" and "Main Street, Hackensack," from *Transfer* #2 (1988); "Why I Am Not a

James Ruggia for "'I woke into another man's day,'" "Meadowlands," "Earth Angel," and "An August Dog"; copyright © by James Ruggia.

David Shapiro and Overlook Press for "Snow" and "Friday Night Quartet, III," from *To an Idea* (Overlook Press, Lewis Hollow Road, Woodstock, N.Y.), copyright © 1983 by David Shapiro; "A Study of Two Late July Fourths" and "The Boy Who Loved Bubbles," from *House (Blown Apart)* (Overlook Press, Lewis Hollow Road, Woodstock, N.Y.), copyright © 1988 by David Shapiro. David Shapiro for "Red Boats," "The Destruction of the Bulwarks at Deal," and "Deal Winter Composition"; copyright © by David Shapiro.

Herschel Silverman and Scrap Paper Review for "Brecht West," "May 5, 1979," and "For Aunt Alta on Her Death," from *Scrap Paper Review Chapbook #1: The Herschel Silverman Issue* (1988). Herschel Silverman for "To Whitman"; copyright © by Herschel Silverman.

Edward R. Smith and Gaede's Pond Press for "Crushed Brown," "Asbury Park," and "I Am That Hero," from *At the Green Pool* (Weehawken, N.J.: Gaede's Pond Press, 1985), copyright © 1985 by Edward Robert Smith, "The Weather," from *Dwasline Road* (Weehawken, N.J.: Gaede's Pond Press, 1983), copyright © 1983 by Edward Robert Smith. Edward R. Smith for "the morning cracks to peeling"; copyright © by Edward Robert Smith.

Elizabeth Anne Socolow for "Driving to Work in New Jersey," from *Footwork* (1988); "The Tack You Take," "To A Friend in Fear," "Lying," and "Bamboo Indoors at the Corporate Center"; copyright © by Elizabeth Anne Socolow.

Madeline Tiger for "The Gull," "The Belleville Girl," "While We Were Thinking of Ginko Leaves," and "Autumn Poem," from *U.S. 1 Worksheets 1987*, copyright © 1987 by Madeline Tiger; "Name and Place," from *I Sing the Song of Myself: An Anthology of Autobiographical Poems*, edited by David Kherdian (New York: Greenwillow, 1978), copyright © 1977 by Madeline Tiger.

Rod Tulloss and From Here Press for "By the Canal Near Griggstown," from *December 1975* (Fanwood, N.J.: From Here Press, 1978), copyright © 1975 by Rod Tulloss. Rod Tulloss for "Drifts," from *Footwork*, (1988), copyright © 1978 by Rod Tulloss; "Seed," copyright © 1983 by Rod Tulloss; "'the peel back,'" from *The Stone #12*, copyright © 1977 by Rod Tulloss; "Error," from *Furtive Notes,*